UNIQUE EATS AND EATERIES

OF

ORLANDO

Library of Congress Control Number: 2018962617
ISBN: 9781681061559

Book Design: Barbara Northcott
Photos credit of the author unless otherwise indicated.

Printed in the United States of America
19 20 21 22 23   5 4 3 2 1

UNIQUE EATS AND EATERIES

OF

ORLANDO

KENDRA LOTT

ROCK SHR

DEDICATION

For Andrew, who always shares his food. And for Lucy,
who always shares her feedback. I love you both every day.

CONTENTS

Acknowledgments IX

Introduction X

East End Market 2

1921 Mount Dora 4

Canvas 6

Hoop-Dee-Doo Musical Revue 8

Audubon Park Community Market 10

Shantell's Just Until 12

Fleet Farming 14

Black Rooster Taqueria 16

Norman's 18

Hot Dog Heaven 20

Athena Roasted Chicken 22

Baggs Produce 24

A Land Remembered 26

Gezellig Cookies 28

Lake Meadow Naturals 30

Taipei 101 32

The Rusty Spoon 34

A Spoon Full of Hope 36

Sandwich Sampler 38

Dandelion Community Café 42

The Goblin Market 44

International Drive 46

Soco Restaurant 48

Citrus 50

Se7en Bites 52

Selam Ethiopian & Eritrean Cuisine 54

Wine Bars 56

Edible Education Experience 58

The Sanctum.. 60

Christner's Prime Steak and Lobster.............................. 62

Strong Water Tavern.. 64

Lakeridge Winery & Vineyards 66

The Meatball Stoppe.. 68

The Tennessee Truffle... 70

Shiraz Market.. 72

Rangoli Sweets 74

Orlando Meats 76

Valhalla Bakery and Valkyrie Doughnuts...................... 78

DaJen Eats Café & Creamery 80

The COOP 82

Disney Springs.. 102

Taste of Chengdu 104

Saba Bakes 106

Long & Scott Farms 108

Coffee for a Cause.. 110

Marshmallows.. 112

Chef Wang's Kitchen 114

1st Oriental Market.. 116

Black Bean Deli... 118

Little Vietnam 120

Victoria & Albert's 122

Winter Garden Farmers Market.............................. 124

Central Florida Ale Trail...................................... 126

Pizza Bruno 128

The Whiskey 130

Hunger Street Tacos 132

Reel Fish Coastal Kitchen + Bar 134

Lee & Rick's Oyster Bar...................................... 136

Kappy's Subs 138

Prato 140

Beefy King 142

The Catfish Place 144

Blueberries 146

DoveCote 150

Neighborhood Markets 152

Maxine's on Shine 154

The Black Hammock 156

Plant Street Market 158

Krungthep Tea Time 160

Caribbean Sunshine 162

Hollerbach's Willow Tree Café 164

Ace Café Orlando 166

Ceviche House 168

Buttermilk Bakery 170

International Food Club 172

Melao Bakery 174

Jimotti's Restaurant 176

Q'Kenan 178

Spicy Girl 180

Sticky Rice Lao Street Food 182

Claddagh Cottage Irish Pub 184

Ararat Euro Food & Bistro 186

The Boheme 188

The Ravenous Pig 190

Capa 192

Reyes Mezcaleria 194

Kadence 196

P Is for Pie Bake Shop 198

Market to Table 200

Whisper Creek Farm 202

Restaurants A to Z 205

Establishments by Neighborhood 209

ACKNOWLEDGMENTS

This book owes a great deal to coffee, but mostly to the people who lent their time and talent to help wrangle the hundreds of photos that appear here. Cathy Agnew, Robert Bangiola, Aaron Van Swearingen, Michael Lothrop, Ashley Coggins, Marta Madigan, and my favorite hand model, Jane Agnew. I couldn't have done it without you.

Friends are always important, but writer friends really, really get it. I'm so grateful for Rona Gindin, Joseph Hayes, Jennifer Greenhill-Taylor, Kristen Manieri, Pam Brandon, Katie Farmand, Bob Morris, and Faiyaz Kara. Thank you for listening.

Hats off to all the chefs and small-business owners who work so hard to bring flavor and flair to a region that some folks are quick to dismiss. As my mother would say, their loss. I am beyond proud to be an Orlandoan and am crossing my fingers for a second edition so I can fall in love with this city's culinary community all over again.

INTRODUCTION

Anyone who's not from the Central Florida area would have a difficult time navigating Orange County's many distinct and diverse neighborhoods. As far as the United States Postal Service is concerned, most of it is just "Orlando," but the city is also home to several official Main Street districts, each with its own historical and cultural flavor. Then there are areas named by developers long before the first house was built, or by immigrants who settled there years later. Many of these neighborhoods' designations are well known by their residents but lost on locals living just a few miles away.

Things were more straightforward when I was growing up in the 1970s. When friends and I asked one another where we were from, we'd say "Spring Oaks" or "River Run," subdivisions in then up-and-coming Seminole County. Dinner out was straightforward too, as everyday choices were limited mostly to chain restaurants or the odd pizzeria, barbecue joint, or Chinese place in a strip mall. Central Florida is still home to plenty of strip malls, but a cursory exploration of any of them may yield West Indian roti, regional Chinese cuisine, or house-made charcuterie. Clearly, straightforward is overrated.

Perhaps the only task more daunting than pinpointing Orlando's communities is defining global ones. For Downtown Orlando's inaugural FusionFest, a two-day street party in 2018, the steering committee divided the globe into ten regions. The goal was for area residents who hailed from each of these regions to share their culture's music, dance, art, and of course food. They came, and for one magical weekend in November, Orlandoans could watch dancers perform the kizomba, learn about traditional Jordanian dress, listen to merengue, and feast on jollof rice, Brazilian barbecue, or Syrian sweets.

Don't wait for a special occasion to enjoy Orlando's wealth of both foreign and familiar culinary delights. While this book is by no means an exhaustive guide—that would require at least a hundred more pages—any given entry might introduce you to a new cuisine, bring you to a new neighborhood, or reacquaint you with a fresh local ingredient. No matter where you start exploring, I hope you'll feel at home.

UNIQUE EATS AND EATERIES
OF
ORLANDO

Orlando's first local food hub

When East End Market opened in 2013, it broke new ground by offering customers an array of artisan foods, flowers, housewares, and handmade goods from small local businesses, all under one roof. Just a stone's throw from Leu Gardens in the Audubon Park Garden District, the market boasts its own botanical bounty, including a working garden that provides produce for several of the merchants and a lush courtyard, where visitors gather even on the rare occasions when the market is closed.

When it's open, look for local and organic fare at Florida & Co. Farm Store. Chef/owner Emily Rankin uses the best of each season's ingredients to craft bright flavors in healthy dishes, such as a Florida Bowl with Jupiter brown rice, salad greens, pickled veggies, and a cilantro-lemongrass sauce with add-ons of Florida wild shrimp, roasted pork, tempeh, or a soft egg.

Farm & Haus delivers weeknight dinners to area residents in addition to serving up breakfast burritos, avocado toast, and chicken biscuits from its corner kiosk. At Hinckley's Fancy Meats, chef Matt Hinckley offers nose-to-tail charcuterie, sausages, and more made the old-fashioned way using heritage breeds.

Hopefuls queue daily for the saucer-sized cookies from Gideon's Bakehouse. Weighing in at just shy of a half-pound, all six flavors—ranging from classic chocolate chip to such seasonal faves as coffee toffee chocolate chip—inevitably sell out before the day's end, hence

> "East End Market is a window into what it means to be an Orlandoan. From bankers to hipsters, young and old, the market is a melting pot of neighbors and visitors."
> – John Rife, owner

Left: Edible gardens at East End Market. Photo by Steven Miller Photography.
Right: The bar at Skyebird. Photo by Steven Miller Photography.

the six-per-person limit. Also made fresh daily are the hand-shaped loaves from Olde Hearth Bread Company, which also provides many of Orlando's best restaurants and finest hotels with scratch classics that are free of preservatives and artificial flavors.

Lineage Coffee Roasting serves its single-origin coffees, cold brew, and espresso from a small nook adjacent to Skyebird, where raw-food fans clamor for organic kombucha, juices, and savory dishes. The cases at La Femme du Fromage are loaded with the finest handcrafted cheeses from the United States and abroad, and DOMU draws dinner and weekend brunch crowds for house-made ramen and other soulful Japanese fare.

The other innovative aspect of East End Market is its culinary incubation program and collaborative kitchen, which continue to foster Orlando's next generation of food entrepreneurs. Having access to affordable kitchen space that they can rent by the hour enables the market's merchants and other local artisans to shift their creative energy away from maintenance and focus on making incredible food.

3201 Corrine Dr.
321-236-3316
eastendmkt.com

Modern Florida cuisine

Mount Dora is a historic lakefront town that has evolved into a charming destination renowned for monthly festivals devoted to everything from art to bicycles to blueberries. Its offerings are eclectic, which is just the way the locals like it and why visitors keep coming back to find something different. 1921 Mount Dora isn't the new kid on the block anymore, but there's always something new on the menu, and while the food here is infused with flavors from other countries, the result feels like Florida.

The restaurant's white brick building is as gracious as the home that it was built to be back in 1921, but now it's filled with works from the Modernism Museum Mount Dora, which sits right across the street. The museum's mission extols the "power of art, craft, and design to ignite the imagination, stimulate thought, and provide enjoyment," and dining among these works does just that. The fusion of the many styles provides a coherent backdrop for the seasonal menu, which reads like a wish list for every fledgling forager.

Executive Chef Josh Oakley, previously of the Smiling Bison in Sanford, brings to 1921 Mount Dora an affinity for seasonal fare and local ingredients, which he prepares with innovation and care. In cooler weather, a crispy duck leg may come with faro, roasted winter vegetables, cranberry, salsa verde, and tamarind. Florida seafood shines in fish tacos dressed with Zellwood sweet corn, on a sandwich topped with slaw and house-made pickles, or in a starter of grilled octopus with a cassoulet made of delicate flageolet beans.

Like all well-raised Southerners, 1921 Mount Dora is always welcoming, but it never seems more so than on Sundays. Brunch is an indulgent affair featuring glazed-ham Benedict, Nashville hot chicken and waffles, and a handful of cocktails sure to put the day in

Left: Ornate gate leading to the chef's table. Photo by Jim Byers courtesy of 1921 Mount Dora.

Top right: Florida octopus with flageolet beans.

Bottom right: Crispy duck leg with farro and roasted winter vegetables. Photo courtesy of 1921 Mount Dora.

proper perspective. The prix fixe menu for Sunday Supper changes weekly but typically showcases comforting entrées, such as chicken fried steak or coq au vin, along with deals on featured bottles from the restaurant's well-curated wine list.

End your experience with a stroll to the water or along Mount Dora's quaint streets and you'll soon find yourself wondering when you might come back.

142 E. Fourth Ave.
352-385-1921
1921mountdora.com

CANVAS

Lakefront restaurant and market

At first glance, Canvas looks like exactly what it is—a sleek yet approachable restaurant, market, and home goods store. Its industrial-chic architecture is a perfect fit for the Lake Nona area, a seven-thousand-acre planned community that sprang to life along with its landmark Medical City in the late aughts. Look more closely, though, and you'll find a menu that pays homage to old Florida's Latin flavors, as well as its Southern roots, with contemporary flair.

The traditional Cuban sandwich is elevated with slow-roasted pork belly and house-cured Canadian bacon. A fried chicken sandwich features bird brined in sweet tea and served with cayenne mayo and house-made pickles. Small plates include sherry-braised octopus, cobia ceviche, and a hearty take on albondigas, a classic Spanish tapa, featuring ground short rib and brisket.

Large plates run the gamut from wild bear Bolognese to beer-battered haddock and chips, but Puerto Rican mofongo, which typically features a mound of deep-fried plantain mash mixed with pork or seafood, is a customer favorite. Here, sautéed shrimp and Roma tomatoes are composed atop a plantain-cilantro fritter in a pool of citrus-saffron broth.

13615 Sachs Ave.
407-313-7800
canvaslakenona.com

Lake Nona is a gigabit community offering Internet speeds two hundred times faster than the average US household.

Top: Canvas exterior. Photo courtesy of Canvas.

Bottom left: Canvas interior. Photo courtesy of Canvas.

Bottom right: Sherry-braised octopus. Photo courtesy of Canvas.

HOOP-DEE-DOO MUSICAL REVUE

Foot stompin' and fried chicken

There are two kinds of people in this world—those who love slapstick vaudevillian comedy and those who don't—and the former will love the Hoop-Dee-Doo. Since 1973 a rotating cast of characters has sung, danced, and do-si-do'd their way around Pioneer Hall in Disney's Fort Wilderness Resort and Campground, which itself is an homage to a simpler time.

The meal served midway through this two-hour experience is simple as well, including limitless silver buckets of smoked ribs and crispy fried chicken; there's even (spoiler alert!) a song about fried chicken. Salad, baked beans, cornbread, and strawberry shortcake round out the fixins and fuel the eager diner through a second act of songs, comedy sketches, and audience participation gags by the game and talented performers.

This is princess-free Disney at its finest and most fun—a timeless but not timeworn show with an energetic and able cast, endless amounts of darn good grub, and 750 acres of pine and cypress forest surrounding the most low-tech resort on Disney property. What's not to love?

4510 N. Fort Wilderness Trail
407-939-3463
disneyworld.disney.go.com/dining/cabins-at-fort-wilderness-resort/hoop-dee-doo-musical-revue

While you're waiting for the show, look for rabbits, deer, armadillos, and other native wildlife on the grounds.

Above: The endless spread at Hoop-Dee-Doo Musical Revue. Photo by David Roark.

Left: The talented cast. Photo courtesy of Disney Photo Imaging.

AUDUBON PARK COMMUNITY MARKET

Monday night meeting place for local food fans

With nonstop sunshine, nearby coasts, and plenty of pasture, it's no surprise that Orlando boasts a bounty of local produce, seafood, meat, dairy, and poultry. And unlike our neighbors in the North, Central Floridians can visit farm markets all year long in more than a dozen spots throughout Orlando and its surrounding counties. But there's only one year-round, weekly market in town where shoppers can be sure of one thing: every bunch of turnips, batch of pickles, bottle of kombucha, or slab of bacon was grown, made, or raised by the person selling it.

Local vendors set up shop in the parking lot of Stardust Video & Coffee (or inside if it rains) to sell fresh produce, baked goods, pastured meats, and wild-caught seafood. Market director Gabby Lothrop ensures that each farmer, artisan, or artist is selling local goods, often visiting farms personally to ensure provenance and sustainable practices. This attention to detail means that locals (and their pets) can simply relax and enjoy the evening, knowing that they're not buying "local" chard purchased from a wholesaler and repackaged. Dirt still clings to the roots of the beets for sale here, and the honey was harvested by the same beekeeper who sits under a ten-by-ten tent and sells it.

Audubon Park Community Market was founded by Orlando native Emily Rankin in 2009.

Left: Paul Tomazin, a.k.a. the Barefoot Farmer, helps a customer. Photo by Michael Lothrop.
Right: Perusing the produce from Fleet Farming. Photo by Michael Lothrop.

Look for insanely pretty produce from Paul Tomazin, a.k.a. the Barefoot Farmer; microgreens and other garden babies from New Growth Urban Farm; hydroponic veggies, raw milk, and cheese from Heart of Christmas Farms; the freshest lettuces and more from Fleet Farming, a bike-powered urban farm that utilizes neighbors' extra lawn space; and pastured free-range chicken and eggs from Azalea Acres Farm among the regular vendors.

Even if you're just in the area to visit, there's plenty to partake in along with the live music and people- and pet-watching. Grab a craft cocktail or beer from the bar at Stardust to pair with Colombian vegan eats from Avenue A Eatery or vegan sweets from CayCakes Bakery. The soaps from Heart Song Naturals only *look* good enough to eat—and with versions made with oatmeal, milk, and honey, it may be tempting to try. Instead, get your breakfast fix with the latest seasonal flavors from Gaia Granola or a fruit-packed snack from Second Breakfast.

1842 E. Winter Park Rd.
audubonmarket.com

SHANTELL'S JUST UNTIL...

Soul food with heart

If life is a numbers game, then Shantell Williams comes out way ahead of most. In 2016 the mother of ten rode her motorcycle across forty-eight states in twenty-seven days to honor her hero, Bessie Stringfield, the first African-American woman to ride solo across the United States. So the fact that her current restaurant is her third location on the same stretch of Sanford Avenue must surely, hopefully mean that the third time is the charm.

The tiny building with big plate-glass windows and cheery bright yellow, silver, and black accents has two entrances. One leads to a small dining area and counter for ordering and the other to a more clubby area with table service and a small stage set up in back. Here, Williams hosts comedy acts, karaoke, a monthly bikers brunch, and steak-and-cigar events, where guests are invited to bring their own whiskey.

On both sides of the place, guests of all ages enjoy unbeatable fried chicken with Southern sides, such as collards, mac-and-cheese, and fried green tomatoes. Her Jamaican, or rather, Jafakin' patties—Williams isn't Jamaican but says a Jamaican lady taught her to make them—ring true, as do her jerked specials, and desserts are as sweet as the sweet tea. Fakin' or not, the rib-sticking fare at this friendly spot should be enough to make this location stick. Just until . . .

Bessie Stringfield was just nineteen when she took her first solo ride across the United States. Her portrait has pride of place in the restaurant.

Shantell Williams.

503 S. Sanford Ave.
407-878-7785

Pedal-powered produce

Whether they care to or not, all householders ultimately learn the ins and outs of lawn care, and with Central Florida's relentless sun, grass farming can be a full-time job. But where some suburbanites just saw a sea of sod, the founders of Fleet Farming spotted an opportunity: farmlettes.

In exchange for a share of the harvest, homeowners in select Orlando neighborhoods set aside a portion of their lawns for farming. Twice per month, groups of volunteers hop on their bikes for a "swarm ride" around each neighborhood to plant, maintain, and harvest the plots, all the while learning the fine art of growing food. The pristine produce is then sold to area restaurants and at the weekly Audubon Park Community Market.

Residents outside the official farmlette zone (or far down on its lengthy wait-list) can hire the experts at Fleet Farming to install raised beds tricked out with timed drip irrigation, soil, seeds, and plants. You'll also get a handy beginner's guide for turning your microfarm into an outdoor grocery store. Those who prefer longer-term edibles can choose a low-maintenance food forest of fruiting trees, such as mango, avocado, and banana.

1030 Kaley Ave.
929-269-3276
fleetfarming.org

Between 2014 and 2018, Fleet Farming converted more that seventy thousand square feet of lawns into working farmland.

Top: Edible garden at a local home. Photo courtesy of Fleet Farming.

Bottom: Volunteers tend a farmlette. Photo courtesy of Fleet Farming.

BLACK ROOSTER TAQUERIA

Farm to taco

If you're looking for a two-fisted burrito stuffed with a kitchen sink of "Mexican" ingredients, you'd best look elsewhere. At this treasure box of a taqueria in the heart of the Mills 50 district, serving sizes are sane, and recipes are authentic, just the way this husband-and-wife team intended.

Owners John and Juliana Calloway get their produce from Florida farms, and the daily catch that Chef John features in the crispy fish taco is from Florida waters. Wine comes from Quantum Leap Winery just across the street, and Florida beers rotate on tap. Bottles of Coca-Cola and Jarritos, however, come from Mexico, as they should.

Tacos, of course, dominate the menu, which changes based on availability, but they're served on organic corn tortillas made by hand, in-house, every single day. Of the nine or so tacos available, only one—the Black Rooster Asada—bears the restaurant's name. Seared beef comes topped with applewood-smoked bacon, Oaxaca cheese, and pickled chili poblano.

Chef John crafted the tables, and Juliana has curated works by local artists to decorate the vibrant, Day-of-the-Dead-inspired interior, which echoes the couple's modern Mexican ethos.

Pozole is a traditional Mexican stew made with hominy. The pozole verde at Black Rooster Taqueria is made with pork shoulder, roasted tomatillos, and serrano chiles.

Top left: The eponymous rooster enjoys pride of place. Photo by Black Rooster Taqueria.

Top right: Tacos, guac, rice, beans, plaintains, and a Mexican Coke. Photo by Black Rooster Taqueria.

Bottom left: Cozy confines. Photo by Black Rooster Taqueria.

Bottom right: Chocolate chipotle flan. Photo by Black Rooster Taqueria.

1323 N. Mills Ave.
407-601-0994
blackroostertaqueria.com

New World cuisine

It's difficult to overstate Norman Van Aken's influence on how the rest of the world perceives—and enjoys—Florida's culinary offerings. Widely regarded as the founding father of New World cuisine, Van Aken is the only Florida chef the James Beard Foundation included in its Who's Who of Food & Beverage in America, a list that the foundation describes as "a cadre of the most accomplished food and beverage professionals in the country."

Starting in the 1970s in Key West and throughout the ensuing decades at his South Florida restaurants, Van Aken has woven local ingredients with flavors from Latin America, Asia, and the Caribbean to create dishes that both evoke and celebrate a sense of place. His namesake restaurant inside the Ritz-Carlton Orlando, which is every bit as upscale as that well-heeled brand would suggest, is as contemporary, elegant, and international as Van Aken's cuisine. Tables in the marble-walled rotunda surround a floor-to-ceiling wine cellar, offering each guest the best seat in the house; the terrace provides views of the resort's tranquil grounds.

Both vantage points provide a beautiful backdrop for Van Aken's menu, where seafood shines in such classics as a cracked-conch chowder spiffed up with saffron and star anise, as well as unexpected creations, such as pan-cooked black grouper with scallion sofrito, sweet-potato agnolotti, romesco sauce, and morita-tomatillo salsa. At many restaurants, filet mignon is a demure dish. Here, it's spiced with guajillo peppers and served with charred shallots, leeks, and the house's version of potatoes a la Huancaina, a traditional Peruvian dish.

Seasonal tasting menus are available with or without pairings from the tome of a wine list, which tips its top hat to newer regions, such as Argentina, Lebanon, and Hungary, along with ample

Above: In the middle of the rotunda. Photo courtesy of Norman's Orlando.

Right: Pork Havana. Photo courtesy of Norman's Orlando.

choices from France, Italy, and California. If your head is spinning like a globe, just ask the sommelier to help you choose whether to pair an Old World wine with New World cuisine. If there's one lesson to take away from Norman's, it's that fusing traditions can result in a beautiful meal.

4012 Central Florida Pkwy.
407-393-4333
ritzcarlton.com/en/hotels/florida/orlando/dining/normans

HOT DOG HEAVEN

Chicago's finest

If there were an award for Most Accurate Restaurant Name, then Hot Dog Heaven would surely win it. Its sign soars higher than most church steeples, its two-pronged fork piercing the heavens as it pierces a fat red frank the size of a pontoon boat. The earthbound portion of the establishment serves a dog-heavy menu that will delight all but vegetarians.

The hot dogs themselves—along with the Polish and Italian sausages—are made by Vienna Beef, which operates not in Vienna but in Chicago, the eden of American charcuterie. This provenance is evident not just in the Chicago swag that decorates the restaurant's walls but also in the prominence and preparation of the menu's chart-topping item: the authentic Chicago hot dog. This proud pup comes in a steamed poppy seed bun topped with mustard, neon green relish, chopped onion, sliced tomato, a pickle spear, and sport peppers. Yes, all on the same bun.

Vienna Beef hot dogs are 100 percent beef with a natural casing, and you can order them here with myriad combinations of cheese (Swiss or American), slaw, kraut, or chili. Crispy and miraculously greaseless fries are the most popular side, but the menu also offers Chicago imports, including Supreme Tamales, Iltaco Pizza Puffs, and Jays potato chips.

Though Hot Dog Heaven opened its doors in 1987, there is an undeniably midcentury vibe. The crisp red-and-white color scheme, the simple yet spot-on menu, and quick but courteous counter staff

> Vienna Beef manufactures more than one hundred million individual hot dogs and Polish sausages each year.

Left: Fork piercing the sky. Photo by Hot Dog Heaven.

Right: A few of the many dogs on the menu. Photo by Hot Dog Heaven.

could make diners of any age feel nostalgic. Indoor seating is sparse, but the covered patio running the length of the exterior has plenty of room for those who'd like a view of busy Colonial Drive. Better still, grab yours to go and head around back and across the street. The gazebo at small-but-sweet Millenium Park is the perfect place to chill out with your chili dog and gaze over Little Lake Barton.

Should you feel so transported by this experience that you begin to dream of operating your very own Chicago hot dog business, Hot Dog Heaven can get you started with its consulting services. After a free fifteen-minute consultation, you can hire the experts to train you in menu and restaurant design, cooking and prep, and even fabrication of a custom hot dog cooker/bun steamer. The perfect name for your restaurant-to-be, however, is up to you.

5355 E. Colonial Dr.
407-282-5746
hotdogheaven.com

ATHENA ROASTED CHICKEN

Rotisserie chicken and Greek specialties

Since 1988, this modest restaurant located in a shopping center in a once quiet corner of Maitland has roasted about one hundred chickens each day. You do the math. Apparently, practice makes perfect because locals still flock here to grab a "home-cooked" chicken dinner to go or a workday lunch on the fly to enjoy within eyeshot of the busy counter or on the peaceful and leafy side patio.

If the name isn't obvious enough, the framed photos of Greece and the abundance of feta cheese, Kalamata olives, and tahini appearing in salads, pita wraps, and sides more than hint at the establishment's proud Greek roots. The window's only neon sign proclaims ROASTED CHICKEN—and the lemon-and-herb-marinated birds do indeed loom large on the menu, in the rotisserie, and in the warming case on the counter—but many Greek favorites have been on the menu for decades, long before buying mass-produced tubs of hummus at every grocery store became the norm. Look for stuffed grape leaves, chicken and rice soup with lemon, tabbouleh salad, gyros, and moussaka, and a comforting casserole of beef, potatoes, and eggplant baked with creamy béchamel sauce. There's also an Americanized but irresistible Greek salad topped with generous slabs of creamy feta, with a few forkfuls of excellent potato salad nestled at the bottom.

> Hummus originated in Egypt in the thirteenth century and crossed over to Greece along with baklava, dolmades, and other "Greek" dishes during their centuries-long trade relationship.

Left: Birds is the word at Athena Roasted Chicken.

Right: A small Greek salad at Athena Roasted Chicken.

Hot and cold sides are available both with a meal and as a meal and include red beans, rice pilaf, green beans, slaw, thick slices of zucchini in tomato sauce, and the same potato salad that makes a cameo in the Greek salad. Roasted potatoes are a fan favorite, and many an online review ponders the secret to their perfection. A touch of cinnamon and a generous hand with the oil are the likely keys to success here.

Chicken that isn't halved or quartered to order for platters is stripped from the bone and topped with varying combinations of sauces (tzatziki, barbecue, red sauce), salads, or melted provolone and served in a grilled pita. In the unlikely event that diners have room for dessert, they can also end on a Greek note with an order of baklava, rice pudding, or tahini cake. If this longstanding family restaurant doesn't transport you to Greece per se, it'll definitely take you back to a time when Maitland was mostly mom-and-pop places just like this one.

487 S. Orlando Ave.
407-539-0669
athenachicken.com

BAGGS PRODUCE

Peanut paradise

To everything there is a season, and the same is true for peanuts. Sure, you can buy them roasted and canned year-round—just look for the dapper dude with the monocle and top hat on the label—but peanuts grow underground and, like all agricultural products, thrive in certain climates. Peanuts like for the soil to be warm, which is why all of the fifteen states in which peanuts are grown commercially are in the southern half of the United States.

Why is this important? Because people who love boiled peanuts know that the only acceptable version is made from green peanuts. Yes, you can make them with hard-shell roasted peanuts, but don't count on being invited back to next week's tailgate party.

Green, or raw, peanuts taste about as pleasant as a raw potato (hence the roasting process) and are far more finicky to boot. When harvested, green peanuts have soft shells and a moisture content ranging from 25 percent to 50 percent, making them highly perishable. They must be kept cool and dry and even then won't last more than a week or so before spoiling. (And spoiled peanuts not only taste terrible but can also make you very sick, even when boiled.) Because this presents challenges for transport, it's uncommon to find green peanuts too far from the farm.

Enter Baggs Produce, a Sanford institution for locally grown Southern staples, such as collards, turnips, mustard greens, shell

> Florida is the second-largest commercial grower of peanuts in the United States, contributing nearly 13 percent to its peanut crop each year.

Left: Okra grows all summer long in Florida.

Center: Raw peanuts are cured but not roasted.

Right: A roadside chalkboard advertises fresh picks.

peas, sweet corn, green tomatoes, sweet onions, rutabaga, and okra. Peanuts are harvested in Florida almost year-round, which means that Baggs has a dependable supply of green peanuts for sale by the pound. Best enjoyed at the beach, while watching the game, or while playing a few rounds of cornhole, this regional delicacy requires little prep besides water, salt, peanuts, and patience. Also, cold beers.

Those who are pressed for time, lack a proper family recipe, or perhaps live with a family member who might complain about the lingering smell of wet peanuts can enjoy Baggs ready-made varieties. Kept hot behind the counter and sold by the scoop, these lovely legumes are available regular (plain or salted) or Cajun (regular or mild). For the timid, the friendly folks on staff suggest combining the regular with the mild Cajun. Hotheads can start with the full-throttle Cajun and never look back.

2485 Sanford Ave.
407-322-3661

A LAND REMEMBERED

Edible homage to Florida history

We can only hope that someday J. D. Salinger's estate will allow someone, anyone to open a delicatessen named for *The Catcher in the Rye*. In the meantime, author Patrick D. Smith's historical novel *A Land Remembered* lives on not just as required reading for Florida's elementary school students but also as the inspiration for a AAA Four Diamond-award-winning restaurant at Rosen Shingle Creek Hotel.

The hotel opened in 2006, nearly 150 years after the fictional Tobias MacIvey arrives in the Florida wilderness. The novel spans three generations and more than a hundred mostly hardscrabble years, but the family's good luck begins with their first successful cattle drive across the state. The treacherous route that Tobias and his crew take is somewhat south of the hotel, but Shingle Creek is considered the headwaters of the Florida Everglades, also a significant setting in the book.

Tobias MacIvey would be out of place in the luxe environs of A Land Remembered, but his wealthy grandson Solomon would surely have enjoyed a starter of alligator and white bean stew or goat cheese fritters with Vidalia onion and tomato jam before tucking into a medium-rare New York strip. Alas, the beef here comes not from the dwindling herds descended from the wild Florida Cracker cattle in the novel but from the more docile and delicious Black Angus.

9939 Universal Blvd.
407-996-1956
landrememberedrestaurant.com

Top: A Land Remembered. Photo courtesy of Rosen Shingle Creek.

Bottom: Chocolate mousse cake. Photo courtesy of Rosen Shingle Creek.

GEZELLIG COOKIES

Dutch tradition with a twist

It took Cassandra Plas five years to perfect her recipe for stroopwafels, or syrup waffles, a traditional Dutch cookie consisting of a layer of caramel sandwiched between two thin cookie layers made from a stiff batter and pressed on a small-gridded waffle iron. It may take you a minute to master the pronunciation of her brand's name (huh-zell-ick), but it'll only take a bite to understand why Plas worked so hard for so long to get it just right.

The owner and chief cookie officer of this nifty niche baking operation since 2015, Plas grew up in Canada eating crispy Dutch cookies, such as coconut macaroons, spicy windmill cookies (speculaas), and rolled, cigar-shaped cookies called kniepertjes, all made by her Dutch oma (grandma). According to Plas, "Our original stroopwafel is a very traditional version of the cookie, while our other flavors—like maple and key lime—reflect where we are from and where we live." Plas also uses ingredients from where she lives, including eggs from Lake Meadow Naturals in Ocoee, and skips the preservatives altogether.

Local restaurants and food purveyors figure into her tasty plan as well. Plas has partnered with Hunger Street Tacos to make the shell for their mezcal ice cream; made ice cream sandwiches with Greenery Creamery, Kelly's Homemade Ice Cream, and DaJen Eats Irie Cream; and provided edges (leftover trimmings after the waffles are cut into circles) for beer making with Ten10 Brewing and

> Stroopwafels were first made in the late eighteenth or early nineteenth century in Gouda, a city in the province of South Holland, the Netherlands.

Left: Cassandra Plas, Gezellig's chief cookie officer. Photo by Steven Miller Photography.
Right: Gezellig stroopwafels pair perfectly with coffee. Photo by Steven Miller Photography.

doughnut toppings with Orlandough. She has also used ingredients from Swine & Sons as well as marshmallow fluff from Sugar Rush Marshmallows at local pop-ups. Says Plas, "We love our local conspirators!"

Boxes of sixteen individually wrapped stroopwafels are available on the website, along with bags of speculaas and kniepertjes. Around town, look for single servings for sale at neighborhood favorites, including East End Market, the Heavy, Bad As's Sandwich, the Bear and Peacock Brewery, Orlando Meats, and Gratitude Coffee. They're also available at local outlets of grocers Lucky's Market and Earth Fare.

No matter where you get your hands on her cookies, Plas hopes that you'll feel some gezellig when you eat them. "Gezellig" is a Dutch word for the feeling you get when you enjoy good atmosphere and good food with people you love, or as Plas says, "It's the warm and fuzzies."

407-637-5121
gezelligcookies.com

LAKE MEADOW NATURALS

Cage-free eggs and poultry

When farmer Dale Volkert was growing up on a family dairy farm in Wisconsin, the relationship between farms and food was obvious. Fast-forward a few decades, and it became equally obvious to Volkert that not many people make that connection easily. So he began inviting friends to bring their children to his farm so they could see for themselves, just like he did when he was a child, and hopefully learn why it's so important for communities to connect the dots.

These days Volkert operates a market on the grounds of his working farm on Lake Meadow, and one trip there is all it takes to understand the value of wholesome food made and grown by people who take pride in producing it. Customers here can see not only the chickens that lay the market's mind-blowingly good eggs—and on Saturdays, children can even gather eggs in the hen house—but also the various breeds of chickens, heritage ducks, and geese, as well as the mini pig, alpacas, sheep, goats, and cattle, that live on the beautifully landscaped grounds.

Inside the market, the shelves, fridges, and freezers are loaded with breads from Olde Hearth Bread Company; seasonal produce from area farms, including nearby Long & Scott Farms; shrimp

> Lake Meadow Naturals supports Slow Food USA, whose members envision a world in which all people can access and enjoy food that is good for them, good for those who grow it, and good for the planet.

Left: Free-range Rhode Island Reds. Photo by Lake Meadow Naturals.

Right: House-made pickles from Lake Meadow Naturals.

from Wild Ocean Seafood Market in Titusville; and the farm's own eggs and poultry. There's also a big selection of hormone-free and non-GMO meats and sausages, Amish butter, premium pastas, whole grains, and quality cheeses from all over the world. The on-site kitchen produces excellent pickles, preserves, dressings, soups, and sauces, as well as a luscious honey butter made only with honey from the farm's own hives, Florida cream, butter, organic cane juice, and a touch of vanilla.

Local chefs know firsthand how much fresher and tastier local products are, which is why so many of them use Lake Meadow Naturals eggs. Chef Kathleen Blake of the Rusty Spoon was the first Orlando chef to work with Volkert, and many other businesses, including artisan bakeries and area resorts, have followed suit. So while it may not matter whether the chicken or the egg came first, it's meaningful to visit the farm where the chicken laid that egg.

10000 Mark Adam Rd.
321-206-6262
lakemeadownaturals.com

Casual spot for Taiwanese food

Just eighteen seats are inside this small family-run storefront near UCF, and most days they're full of locals looking for a taste of Taiwan. On this mountainous island just a hundred miles off the coast of China, those tastes often come in the form of soups, stews, and snacks, and the menu here reflects that. There's an entire section dedicated to lu wei, or dishes braised in soy sauce, as well as hearty snacks, such as a steamed bun with braised pork belly that's practically a meal in itself.

If some of the available dishes don't strike you as Taiwanese—orange chicken, ramen, and the ubiquitous chicken named after a fictional general—it's because they aren't. Taiwanese cooking has been influenced by many cultures, and Taiwanese people like to mix it up as much as anyone. Not to mention that it never hurts to have a few familiar dishes to appease the less adventurous diner. (The timid should likewise be unafraid of spice; even "spicy" Taiwanese food is not at all incendiary.)

If authentic fare is what you're after, though, the staff will happily point you in the right direction. Beef noodles are such a national obsession in Taiwan that there's an annual festival devoted to them. Niu rou tang mian, the classic spicy beef noodle soup, is on the main menu, and beef with noodles in spicy peppercorn sauce is a regular on the specials board behind the counter. The specials board is also

Shelves under the restaurant's glass-topped tables are stocked with current issues of Chinese-language newspapers, as well as the odd outdated copy of *Food & Wine*.

Left: Diners can catch up on the latest food trends or Asian news items while they wait.
Right: Three cups chicken is a customer favorite.

the place to find fresh seafood dishes, such as noodles with shrimp or oyster and pork chitterlings or a thick stew made with squid and shiitake mushrooms.

Another favorite Taiwanese dish is three cups chicken, which is chunks of boneless dark meat braised in a mixture of equal parts soy sauce, rice wine, and sesame oil along with whole garlic cloves, ginger, and fresh basil. Legend has it that the recipe, which originated in what is now Beijing but has evolved into Taiwan's national dish, was created in 1283 by a prison warden using the few ingredients on hand to prepare a last meal on the eve of a prisoner's execution. Here, it's available as a meal box and served with the day's soup, steamed rice, noodles, minced pork, a side of seasonal vegetables, a braised egg, and a slice or two of garlicky house-made sausage.

3050 Alafaya Tr., Oviedo
407-542-1528
facebook.com/taipei101

THE RUSTY SPOON

Downtown gastropub

You can call chef/owner Kathleen Blake's restaurant farm-to-table, but she'll be the first one to tell you that's just the way she's always cooked. From helping her grandmother make family dinner on Sundays to stints as chef de cuisine at Restaurant Nora in DC and at Melissa Kelly's Primo at the JW Marriott Orlando, Grande Lakes, Blake learned to let high-quality ingredients shine through and elevate simply prepared dishes. At her own restaurant, which she and her husband, William, opened in the historical Church Street District in 2011, her seasonal menu starring Florida produce and proteins taught Orlandoans to love local long before it became commonplace.

As the first Orlando chef to use eggs from Lake Meadow Naturals, the Iowa native continues to give them pride of place on her menu, both in stuffed variations, such as "red devil" with Tabasco, herbs, cornichons, and oven-dried tomatoes, and as the soft-cooked *pièce de résistance* atop a salad of seasonal greens with sautéed chicken livers and warm bacon vinaigrette. Always an advocate for nose-to-tail butchering, Blake also makes occasional use of grilled chicken hearts as a tasty skewered snack.

Blake serves primarily sustainable seafood caught in Florida, and it appears in such dishes as the "dirty South," a mélange of Cape Canaveral shrimp, little-neck clams, and the day's freshest catch in

The Rusty Spoon is within walking distance of the Dr. Phillips Center for Performing Arts, the Amway Center, and the SunRail station, making this popular spot even more packed on game and show nights.

Left: Lake Meadow Naturals red devil stuffed eggs. Photo by The Rusty Spoon.
Right: Utterly addictive shoestring fries. Photo by The Rusty Spoon.

a shrimp-peanut broth with garlicky greens and heirloom grits. The seasonal crudité plate and "chef's whim" butcher's plate with house-made condiments (Blake's staff calls her the Pickle Queen) change daily, but guests can always count on the "55," a half-pound grass-fed beef burger stuffed with bacon and Gruyère, smothered with onions, and dressed with aioli and house pickles on a soft roll.

Blake is well loved not only for her food, which was honored with James Beard Award nominations in 2013 and 2015, but also for her dedication to the local culinary community. She is active in the James Beard Foundation's efforts to advance women in the culinary industry, and in 2018 won the Beacon Award from the Foodservice Council for Women in honor of her support of women in foodservice. So call her ethos farm-to-table if you will, but Blake's influence reaches far beyond Rusty's dining room.

55 W. Church St.
407-401-8811
therustyspoon.com

A SPOON FULL OF HOPE

Groceries for good

As the primary food source for 550 nonprofit feeding programs, Second Harvest Food Bank of Central Florida has a lot on its plate. In 2017 it distributed nearly fifty-eight million meals to partner programs, such as food pantries, soup kitchens, women's shelters, senior centers, day-care centers, and after-school programs. And as if that wasn't enough, it also hosts a tuition-free sixteen-week culinary training program to help qualified, economically disadvantaged adults learn the culinary and life skills necessary for a food-service career.

More than 250 students completed training between 2013 and 2018, and every single one graduated with a paying job. In 2018 Second Harvest created a signature food line to support the program, and you can help just by purchasing a jar of honey, a pint of soup, or some shortbread cookies from A Spoon Full of Hope.

Second Harvest chef Jill Holland created the tomato-basil Soup for Good using quality ingredients and no preservatives; it's packaged in Winter Springs. The Honey for Good line includes raw, unfiltered orange blossom, palmetto, and wildflower honeys from Orlando's

---

In 2009 Florida enacted the first legislation in the nation requiring that honey processed, produced, or sold in the state must be a "natural food product resulting from the harvest of nectar by honeybees."

A SPOON FULL OF

HOPE

a product of
SECOND HARVEST FOOD BANK
OF CENTRAL FLORIDA

Above: A Spoon Full of Hope: Chef Robert Pagen, Chef Israel Santiago, Chef John Dizon, and Chef Jill Holland.

Left: Every item produced by A Spoon Full of Hope carries this logo.

Goldenrod Apiaries; mangrove honey hails from Jester Bee Company in Mims, and Cookies for Good are made with real butter. So, good things do come in small packages and, sometimes, jars.

aspoonfullofhope.org

SANDWICH SAMPLER

World flavors on the go

Hot or cold, hoagie or grinder, sub or panini, Orlando is a city with serious sandwich game, and because Central Floridians are a diverse lot, some of the best sandwich-centric eateries deliver international flavors in down-home digs.

Aficionados may argue about whether the Cuban sandwich originated in Miami or Tampa, but most agree that the essential element is authentic Cuban bread, which is flatter and has a thinner crust than a French baguette. Add to that a mix of ham, roasted pork, Swiss cheese, mustard, and pickles and, presto, you've got yourself a fine lunch! Orlando's spots for classic Cuban sandwiches—regardless of their origins—are spot-on.

Central Floridians have also had a long love affair with the banh mi, a Vietnamese creation involving a crisp French baguette slathered with butter and often pâté, then layered with combinations of charcuterie or thinly sliced grilled meats and dressed with cilantro, pickled carrots, and pickled daikon. Banh mi has strayed to menus beyond the Little Saigon area of Mills 50, where many Orlandoans got their first taste of Vietnamese cuisine, but some of the best versions are still found there.

History holds that the small loaves used for Mexican tortas— the oval bolillo and the slightly larger, rounder telera—are also descendants of the baguette. Stuffed with endless variations of cold cuts, braised or fried meat, beans, and cheese and topped with lettuce, mayo, and tomato, these hearty handhelds satisfy.

A few newer sandwich spots riff on the classics to create original combos or use flavors from traditional non-sandwich dishes and press them between bread. Either way, you'll be impressed with the results.

Crunchy chicken from AJ's Press.

TRY IT

Cuban Sandwiches to Go is exactly what it sounds like. Cash only.
1605 Lee Rd.
407-578-8888
cubansandwichestogo.com

Banh Mi Nha Trang offers an array of banh mi from a small
storefront in the back of a Mills 50 plaza. Cash only.
1216 E. Colonial Dr.
407-346-4549
facebook.com/banhminhatrang

Tortas el Rey is a walk-up with tortas al pastor and more fit for a king.
6151 S. Orange Blossom Tr.
407-850-6980
tortas-el-rey.com

Above: Cuban pride at Cuban Sandwiches to Go.

AJ's Press serves crunchy chicken, beer-braised brisket, Cuban combos, and more on locally baked bolillo and telera rolls.
182 W. SR 434, Longwood
407-790-7020
ajspresslongwood.com

Bad As's Sandwich is a casual counter with house-made sandwich fillings, including crispy Asian glazed pork belly, shaved beef, adobo pork, and fried cod.
207 N. Primrose Dr.
407-757-7191
badasssandwiches.com

Top: The Porkalypse at Bad As's Sandwich. Photo by Juan Benavides.

Bottom: Courtyard of the small plaza that is home to Banh Mi Nha Trang. Photo by AaronVan.

DANDELION COMMUNITY CAFÉ

Mills 50 haven for fun veg fare

The name of this groovy green 1920s bungalow says it all. It's most certainly a café where you can order a variety of organic teas and tisanes to enjoy in one of the three tiny dining rooms or on the gracious patio. There's also a selection of juices and kombucha bottled in Florida, along with craft beer and wine and, of course, a full menu of sandwiches, soups, wraps, bowls, and smaller nibbles. But it's the community part of the name that really rings true at the café affectionately known as Dandy.

Outside, green space connects the café to the neighboring Florida School of Holistic Living, whose staffers maintain a community garden of medicinal herbs. Inside Dandy, works from local artists are on display and on sale, and signage promotes on-site evenings of spoken word, live music, and moon circles. The customers chatting with the counter staff or waiting for their orders to arrive all seem to know one another, making for a relaxed but lively vibe even for first-time diners.

New visitors will find plenty of reasons to come back and sample the kitchen's diverse and wholesome creations. Beans, greens, and grains are the menu's anchors, but chef Mark Thompson's creative plating, thoughtful sauces, and seasonal produce from local farms, such as Frog Song Organics and New Growth Urban Farm, keep dishes fresh and lively. Chickpea of the Sea, a savory "tuna" salad made with chickpeas, comes with a house blend of grains, lettuces, or both, along with fresh and house-pickled local veggies, barbecued pumpkin seeds, and scratch ranch dressing. The kitchen also makes its own kimchi when local Napa cabbage is available and serves it

Top left: All veg all day at Dandelion Café. Photo by Azuree Wiitala.

Top right: Chef Mark Thompson in the garden at Dandy. Photo by Azuree Wiitala.

Bottom: You'll always know where you are at Dandelion Café. Photo by Azuree Wiitala.

with cucumbers, mung bean sprouts, carrots, cilantro, cashews, and the house's "gingerous" dressing.

Other kitchen experiments are perpetually in the works, but a key element will remain unchanged: more than 90 percent of the ingredients used here are organic, and none contain animal products. Dandy also purchases local items whenever possible (including artisan breads from Olde Hearth Bread Company), selects fair-trade products, and offers loads of options that are low in or free from gluten. Thankfully, Dandy will never be free from fun, awesome menu puns and a constantly growing and diverse community.

618 N. Thornton Ave.
407-362-1864
dandelioncommunitea.com

THE GOBLIN MARKET

Home away from home

If there's one thing the management at the Goblin Market can count on, it's loyalty, from both their staff and their customers. Many regulars have been coming to this locally owned restaurant since day one, and they're rewarded not only with many of the same perfectly executed dishes that have been on the menu since its inception but also with seamless service from veteran servers, some of whom have worked here for nearly two decades.

It's easy to understand the staying power of this charming place, a 1950s home that was remodeled in 1996 for the restaurant's debut. With three book-lined dining rooms, a handsome wooden bar, and polished yet soothing decor, the homey setting delights diners as much as the familiar fare does. At lunchtime, a pecan-curry chicken avocado salad is a star of the garden, while the grill puts out a decadent beef burger with truffle and mushroom béchamel or a zingy lamb burger with green harissa and feta aioli. Dinner entrées combine domestic ingredients with international flair in such dishes as blackened Florida snapper with sauce Veracruz.

The kitchen is loyal to local purveyors and sources ingredients from many area farms, including Zenn Naturals and Frog Song

Tempura artichoke hearts are a fan favorite and the only appetizer to appear on both the lunch and dinner menus. They're stuffed with pesto cream cheese and served with sweet-and-hot mustard.

Left: Book-lined dining room. Photo by the Goblin Market.

Top right: Lamb burger with green harissa, feta aioli, and arugula. Photo by the Goblin Market.

Bottom right: Pecan-curry chicken salad with avocado. Photo by the Goblin Market.

Organics for produce and Lake Meadow Naturals for fresh meats and eggs. The restaurant also serves single-origin locally roasted coffee from Wild Bear Coffee in nearby Tavares.

330 Dora Drawdy Way, Mount Dora
352-735-0059
goblinmarketrestaurant.com

INTERNATIONAL DRIVE

Global tables

Since the famous Mouse opened for business in 1971, Central Floridians have kept pace with the tourists who love all things theme park. With Florida resident rates and annual passes making entry more affordable, it's commonplace for Orlandoans to make a day of it at Diagon Alley or eat and drink around the world at Epcot. Even the resorts at Universal and Disney have long counted their fair share of area residents among the guests enjoying a date-night dinner or sipping and strolling during special food and wine events.

International Drive, however, has been slower to garner that local love, especially among diners. The 11.1-mile thoroughfare is as packed with fast-food chains, souvenir shops, and hotels as it is with cars, and most of the sit-down restaurants have long catered primarily to tourists on a budget or conventioneers on an expense account. In the past decade, however, several restaurants have opened that have attracted positive attention from area residents and critics alike, and there's also been a renewed interest in a handful of finds that have been hiding in plain sight all along.

After all, what other street in Orlando boasts restaurants where you can cook Japanese hot pot at your table, eat spicy doro wat on a spongy layer of injera bread that covers the table, or sip retsina and watch a belly dancer shimmy on top of your table? If you haven't already, it's time to give I-Drive a try.

> In 1968 Orlando attorney Finley Hamilton paid $90,000 for the ten acres of palmetto scrub that would become the first stretch of International Drive.

Left: Seafood paella from Tapa Toro. Photo by Bartlett Image.

Right: Servers make it rain during nightly belly dancing. Photo courtesy of Taverna Opa.

TRY IT

Taverna Opa offers a large selection of Greek mezze, entrées, and wines, along with nightly belly dancing, in seriously festive environs at Pointe Orlando.
9101 International Dr.
407-351-8660
opaorlando.com

Tapa Toro is the place to go for creative Spanish tapas, classic paella served family style, and nightly flamenco dancing at ICON Orlando 360.
8441 International Dr.
407-226-2929
tapatoro.restaurant

Nile Ethiopian Restaurant has been delighting tourists, locals, and critics with authentic Ethiopian fare in a warm and welcoming environment since 2006.
7048 International Dr.
407-354-0026
nileorlando.com

Hanamizuki is a serene spot for traditional Japanese sushi, ramen, hot pot, and grilled specialties.
8255 International Dr.
407-363-7200
hanamizuki.us

SOCO RESTAURANT

Southern contemporary cuisine

Chef Greg Richie may not be from Orlando—the Texas native moved here in 2000 to become the executive chef/partner at Roy's Orlando after working at chef Roy Yamaguchi's original restaurant in Hawaii—but he has grown to love it. After taking over the kitchen at Emeril Lagasse's Tchoup Chop at the Loews Royal Pacific Resort at Universal Orlando, Richie moved on in 2006 to stake his culinary claim on a lively corner of Orlando's Thornton Park.

At once Southern (so) and contemporary (co), Soco's menu has a Southern sensibility that Richie honed during his early years working in renowned restaurants in Charleston and Atlanta and fuses with a largely Floridian larder. Chicken and fresh eggs come from Lake Meadow Naturals in Ocoee, Jupiter rice is grown and processed in Jacksonville at Congaree and Penn, and McGregor's Greens in Apopka is a source for microgreens and herbs.

Richie typically has a slightly lighter (and always creative) take on the Southern classics that his kitchen makes from scratch, such as his favorite Soco-style "chicken and dumplings." In this small plate, slices of chicken are served with lobster dumplings, local mushrooms, and edamame in a delicate soy butter. Other small plates of boiled-peanut hummus and oysters crisped in cornmeal and served with pickled green-tomato relish are perfect for sharing.

Hearty grilled meatloaf with lobster mashed potatoes vies for fan-fave status with Korean-style fried chicken. Richie shows his Southern side in veg-friendly dishes, such as handmade ravioli with

Soco's popular Sunday brunch does not hold back on carbs. Look for such whimsical creations as homemade Pop-Tarts, "everything bagel" biscuits, and skillet cornbread.

Top left: Chef Greg Richie. Photo courtesy of Soco.

Bottom left: Golden beets and fennel salad with duck confit and candied nuts. Photo courtesy of Soco.

Right: Micro-chives from a local grower. Photo courtesy of Soco.

smoked black-eyed peas and a chicken-fried cauliflower "steak." Carnivores and vegans alike can enjoy an array of clever cocktails and one of the best whiskey lists in town.

Richie has been in Orlando long enough to appreciate the significance of the growing local food movement and is a proud member of local groups, as well as national ones like the Southern Food Alliance, that support it. Says Richie, "We are very proud to be a part of the amazing food culture that is exploding in Central Florida," and Orlando is proud to have him.

629 E. Central Blvd.
407-849-1800
socothorntonpark.com

The Sunshine State's most iconic export

Citrus may be heart healthy, but growing it is not for the faint of heart. Freezes, hurricanes, and pathogens have plagued the industry since commercial growing in Florida began in the late 1880s. Florida citrus production reached its apex during the 1971–72 growing season, when the harvest surpassed two hundred million boxes for the first time. In the 2015–16 season, however, production hovered just above ninety-four million boxes. This is largely attributed to the loss of acreage from citrus greening disease, which spread from one to thirty-three counties in less than five years during the mid aughts, and the industry has yet to recover from the losses it incurred during Hurricane Irma in 2017.

Long story short: enjoy delicious Florida citrus while you still can.

The primary varieties of oranges grown in Florida are navel, Hamlin, pineapple, ambersweet, and Valencia; the most prevalent grapefruit varieties are ruby red, flame, Thompson, Marsh, and Duncan. The growing season for grapefruit and oranges starts in September and October, respectively, and runs through June, with different varieties available at varying times. Hybrids, such as the honeybell (the industry trade name for a Minneola tangelo, which is a cross between a Dancy grapefruit and a Duncan tangerine) and its cousin the Orlando tangelo (a Dancy tangerine crossed with a Duncan grapefruit), are favored by aficionados for their juiciness and intensely sweet flavor and fragrance.

Faculty from the University of Florida have helped a number of Florida citrus growers diversify—it just so happens that certain blueberry varietals take to soil where citrus trees used to grow—and there are still a handful of family-owned growing and packing operations in the Central Florida area that you can visit. When you do, be sure to thank them for their hard work.

Left: Hollieanna's Maitland packinghouse. Photo by Robert Bangiola.

Right: Tangerines and tangelos for sale at Hollieanna. Photo by Robert Bangiola.

TRY IT

Hollieanna Groves has been packing and shipping Florida citrus since 1954. The Lingle family operates a farm store at their historic packinghouse from November through April and sells freshly squeezed juice along with the citrus, honey, and other gifts available online.

540 S. Orlando Ave., Maitland

407-644-8803

hollieanna.com

White's Red Hill Groves was established in the Conway area of Orlando in 1962. All operations for their gift citrus business now take place at their grove in Sanford; the farm store operates year-round and offers u-pick berries, herbs, barbecue sandwiches, and ice cream.

7218 Ronald Reagan Blvd., Sanford

407-885-0272

redhillgroves.com

Showcase of Citrus offers u-pick citrus in season and monster truck rides through the groves all year long. Established in 1989, the 2,500-acre estate cultivates and sells fifty varieties of citrus.

5010 US Hwy. 27, Clermont

352-394-4377

showcaseofcitrus.com

SE7EN BITES

Southern fare and nostalgic sweets

At this lively lime-green building near downtown, you can have your cake, eat it too, and have enough left over to share with a friend. You may even have met that friend in the line that often snakes around said building, a testament to the popularity of this Orlando outpost for breakfast, brunch, biscuits, and baked goods.

Locals have embraced chef/owner Trina Gregory-Propst's heartfelt hospitality and way with butter since she opened Se7en Bites in 2013. She and her wife, Va Propst, moved the business a few blocks east into a much bigger venue in the fall of 2016, and crowds have continued to fill the space for breakfast, brunch, and lunch, which Gregory-Propst says are "the three best meals of the day."

Her loyal customers agree and gladly queue for their chance to enjoy items from the breakfast and lunch menus, which are served all day, every day. Think buttermilk-garlic biscuits topped with pimiento cheese, egg, and ham, bacon, or sausage; five-cheese mac n cheese topped with onion béchamel and a bacon and potato-chip crumble; or one of the weekend brunch specials, such as "Colonel Marmalade in the Kitchen with a Knife," that Gregory-Propst whips up to entertain the regulars.

Signature sweets are clearly a huge draw as well, and while it was the Vanilla Bean Bourbon Bacon Moon Pie that made its star turn on Guy Fieri's *Diners, Drive-Ins and Dives*, Gregory-Propst's

> Gregory-Propst had a sleeve gastrectomy in 2007 and afterward was allowed seven bites per meal. She named her business Se7en Bites in honor of making each bite the best one ever.

Left: Plant City strawberries and rosewater Chantilly top a pink-peppercorn sweet shortbread biscuit. Photo courtesy of Se7en Bites.

Right: Owner Trina Gregory-Propst. Photo courtesy of Se7en Bites.

personal favorite is her coconut cream pie. "It is my grandmother's recipe and the same one she would make me every year for my birthday," she says. Whether she's using her grammy's recipe or her own, Gregory-Propst executes each item from scratch using the same thoughtfully chosen ingredients, including Plant City strawberries in season, orange-blossom honey from Apopka, and the 72 percent dark chocolate chips she uses in her chocolate chip cookies "to balance the sweet."

That sense of balance is what enables Gregory-Propst and her staff to keep customers happy even when lines are long and favorites run out, as they often do. She also finds the time to cater weddings and other celebrations, and to participate in area charity events and give back to the community she loves. And they love her—and her chicken pot pies—right back.

617 N. Primrose Dr.
407-203-0727
se7enbites.com

SELAM ETHIOPIAN & ERITREAN CUISINE

Tradition and spice all rolled up

A traditional Ethiopian coffee ceremony can take up to ninety minutes, a relatively short amount of time considering that Ethiopians were the first to discover, centuries ago, how to turn this previously disregarded fruit into the drink that fuels nations today. Here in this tranquil azure dining room in the corner of a Williamsburg strip mall, it is a much shorter but still delightful coda to a relaxing meal that is steeped in tradition.

Most Ethiopian and Eritrean restaurants—the now neighboring countries were one until the early 1990s, and their cuisines may seem nearly identical to a first-time diner—focus on the same dishes that their countrymen have loved for generations, and the menu here echoes those options. Look for a variety of wats made from beef, lamb, or chicken stewed in a thick sauce seasoned with berbere; tibs, meat, or mushrooms sautéed with spices, onions, and other vegetables; kitfo, a dish of spiced lean beef served tartare style (or to desired doneness) with house-made soft cheese; and an array of delicately spiced vegetarian dishes made of lentils, split peas, collards, and more.

Whether you sit at a conventional table or—as per the custom in Ethiopia and Eritrea—in low seats around a round table that serves

> Berbere is not a spice in itself but a spice blend typically consisting of ground chilies, ginger, coriander, cloves, cinnamon, nutmeg, and others at the discretion of the cook.

Left: Low seats around a communal platter are traditional in Ethiopia and Eritrea.
Right: Rolls of injera for scooping up kitfo and doro wat.

as a shared platter, entrées are served on top of a spongy mat of injera bread, with extra roll-ups on the side for scooping up morsels of food with your hands. While this style of eating was likely born out of necessity, it does lend itself to the convivial feeling of sharing a meal here, as do sips of tej, an Ethiopian honey wine.

Coffee is a similarly laid-back affair, at least for guests. Servers roast coffee beans in a shallow pan until the beans are slightly blackened. Then they bring the pan out to the dining room so that each guest can soak in the aroma of the roasting beans along with burning incense. They then add the ground beans to hot water in a long-necked clay pot called a jebana and pour it tableside into delicate cups. Custom dictates that each guest enjoy three cups before leaving the table and the company of your hosts. The choice is yours, of course, but once you've enjoyed a cup or three of this restaurant's hospitality you'll likely return for more.

5494 Central Florida Pkwy.
407-778-3119
ethiopianrestaurantorlando.com

WINE BARS

Grapes by the glass

Orlando's culinary community is well known for its talent, and chefs have garnered recognition from local critics as well as nominations for James Beard Awards. Restaurant wine lists have also racked up praise from the likes of *Wine Spectator*, with a handful of fine-dining establishments receiving its Award of Excellence each year. But thanks to a growing number of small but well-curated wine bars that have begun to pop up all over Central Florida, you can try a myriad of interesting wines from both established and emerging producers without committing to a whole bottle.

The area's most notable wine bars have sprung up within the past five years, and according to Judith Smelser, the local journalist and wine aficionado behind the popular Orlando Wine Blog, "Their existence is crucial to the Orlando wine community's growing sophistication." When you visit, don't look for "predictable" offerings from Napa and Bordeaux. Instead, Smelser encourages customers to trust these knowledgeable owners and try something unfamiliar. Says Smelser, "These establishments are run by young wine professionals with a passion for pushing the envelope and finding approachable ways to encourage their patrons to explore and revel in the amazing diversity the world of wine has to offer."

So get out there and swirl, sip, and repeat. After you find your favorite glass, you may spring for the bottle after all.

Left: The bar at the Parkview. Photo by Robert Bangiola.

Right: By the bottle or the glass at Digress. Photo by Jade Apisuk.

TRY IT

Digress is a relaxed neighborhood wine bar and bottle shop with an indoor lounge, an outdoor patio, an indoor cellar for private gatherings, and regular pop-ups by food truck Smoke & Donuts.
1215 Edgewater Dr.
407-426-7510
digresswine.com

Swirlery Wine Bar is also a retail shop and tasting room featuring selections by certified sommelier Melissa J. McAvoy, who owns and runs the artsy space with her partner, DJ Damian "Collaborator" Roman.
1508 E. Michigan Ave.
407-270-6300
swirlery.com

Luisa's Cellar is a wine bar and coffee shop that also offers a large craft beer and vinyl selection, as well as regular live music, pairing events, and classes.
206 Sanford Ave., Sanford
407-915-7309
facebook.com/luisascellar

The Parkview is the only one in this group to offer a full (and full-time) menu and is a popular spot on Tuesdays for trivia night.
136 S. Park Ave., Winter Park
407-647-9103
theparkviewwp.com

EDIBLE EDUCATION EXPERIENCE

Community kitchen house and culinary garden

It all started as an edible garden on the campus of Orlando Junior Academy run by a parent volunteer named Brad Jones. Teachers gradually began to integrate lessons from the garden into the classroom, and in 2011 local chefs/instructors Kevin Fonzo and Sarah Cahill began to teach cooking classes to students in fifth through eighth grades. In 2017 the Emeril Lagasse Foundation Kitchen House & Culinary Garden opened right across the street.

Now OJA's students are able to hone their skills in a fully tricked-out kitchen with room for everyone—and even an upstairs gallery for observers—but they're not the only ones to benefit from this incredible resource. During one-day workshops and weeklong summer camp sessions, children from all over Central Florida come to learn about the garden's bounty from Jones and harvest it to make delicious plant-based meals under the watchful eye of chef/instructor Allyson Van Lenten. Adults can get in on the fun during regular Chef Night events, when area chefs teach guests how to cook signature dishes, and at La Tavola, Chef Fonzo's regular pop-up dinners featuring the Italian dishes he loves most.

No matter what event you attend, you'll walk away with greater appreciation for the journey that our food takes from plant to plate

Top left: A father and son enjoy learning together at a Chef's Night event. Photo by Jeffrey Onore.

Bottom left: Young chefs learn new skills at summer camp. Photo by Jeffrey Onore.

Right: Harvesting pineapple at summer camp. Photo by Jeffrey Onore.

and enjoy the results in a communal and convivial atmosphere with people who are eager to learn.

26 E. King St.
edibleed.org

Real, damn good food

It says so right on the door to the Sanctum, a tiny haven for all things vegan (and all things coffee) in a small strip mall not far from busy Colonial Drive. The food is real, and it's damn good—in equal amounts. Not content to serve merely "healthy" food, chef/owner Chelsie Savage describes her menu as "a celebration of plants and health-promoting ingredients. We take foods that are good for you, put them front and center, and make people fall in love with them."

And love them they do. The space has been a huge hit since the self-taught chef and her husband, Jamie, opened for business in 2016 after many years of traveling throughout the United States to try plant-based foods. Her creations have struck a chord with the many area residents yearning for a new plant-based restaurant option and with people who simply want good food.

That food takes the form of not only bowls, burritos, and salads—including Savage's fave, the Shiva Salad with butternut squash, organic kale, sweet apples, and candied walnuts, all smothered in a curry peanut dressing—but also in sophisticated pasta preparations and dinner-only entrées. The Southern Soul with herbed mushroom gravy, black-eyed pea tempeh, organic potato, sweet potato, organic brown rice or quinoa, organic beans, spicy mustard quick slaw, organic house-made tempeh, broccoli, and grit cake makes for a satisfying supper.

The Sanctum also does a brisk business in cold-pressed juice, smoothies, tea, and coffee, which it sources locally from Golden Hills Coffee Roasters. Locally made kombucha from Living Vitalitea is available on its own or in a cocktail, such as the Chelsie, which blends 'buch with a spicy ginger-and-turmeric shot and dry sparkling wine.

Left: Lattes made with espresso, matcha, or turmeric. Photo by Olivia Bennet.

Top right: Real, damn good food at the Sanctum. Photo by Olivia Bennet.

Bottom right: The Sanctum's French toast casserole. Photo by Olivia Bennet.

Savage also sources as much as possible from local vendors, such as Frog Song Organics and Sugar Top Farms. "Their produce can often be found highlighted in our seasonal specials that rotate weekly," Savage said. She also buys baby greens from Fleet Farming, which are grown on neighborhood lawns, delivered by bicycle, and often served the same day they are picked.

All that good food must keep the Savages healthy. The Sanctum's sister concept, Proper & Wild, opened in late 2018 in nearby Winter Park.

715 N. Fern Creek Ave.
407-757-0346
thesanctumcafe.com

CHRISTNER'S PRIME STEAK AND LOBSTER

Timeless favorites, family ownership

The busy commercial stretch of Lee Road between I-4 and Edgewater Drive isn't an obvious spot for a high-end steakhouse. Sandwiched between affluent Winter Park and College Park, it wasn't notably nicer in 1993, when Russ and Carole Christner opened their Bakerstreet Grill here, but several years, concept changes, and major renovations later, the Christner family still operates a neighborhood restaurant with a pride of ownership—and pride of place—that comes through with every meal.

From the handsome porte cochère at the entrance to the dimly lit dining room lined with tufted burgundy leather banquettes, Christner's Prime Steak and Lobster isn't just all the rage on Lee Road. It attracts all of Orlando and beyond. USDA prime beef is the star of the show here, but guests also clamor for the hubcap-sized onion rings and decadent lobster macaroni and cheese. Cold-water lobster tails are carved tableside and served simply with drawn butter and lemon, and servers are happy to help guests navigate the 4,500-bottle wine list. Service is formal but friendly, largely because so many staffers have worked for the Christners for years.

For a truly only-in-Orlando evening, visit on Saturdays from 7:00 to 9:00 when professional magicians perform tableside.

729 Lee Rd.
407-645-4443
christnersprimesteakandlobster.com

Top: David, Alice, Carole, Ellen, and Claire Christner. Courtesy of Christner's Prime Steak and Lobster.

Bottom: Elegant environs. Courtesy of Christner's Prime Steak and Lobster.

STRONG WATER TAVERN

Rum flights and Caribbean tapas

Just beyond the stylish lobby at Loews Sapphire Falls Resort at Universal Orlando, this island-inspired watering hole overlooks the resort's lagoon and sits under vaulted ceilings depicting vintage maritime maps of the Caribbean. The real eye candy, however, is the wall of vintage rums, which foreshadows the beautiful and boozy experience to come.

More than one hundred different rums are available here, and the list is divided into several categories, primarily by history. The list's lengthy intro details the evolution of rum, from sugar cane to the Age of Exploration on through to Colonial America, when rum consumption declined as the population moved west and began to favor grain-based spirits. Fortunately for rum fans, Prohibition-era tourists flocked to the islands and fell in love with rum all over again, and today production flourishes not just in the islands but also in Florida.

With so many rums to choose from, you'll welcome assistance from a rum captain, a.k.a. rum sommelier, a.k.a. your new favorite person. These knowledgeable guides can help you embark on a personalized rum-tasting journey by way of one of the menu's many flights, cocktails, punches, or tots (house-infused rum shots paired with soda or beer backs). There are elevated versions of classic drinks, such as a proper (i.e., shaken, not frozen) daiquiri or mules with house-made ginger beer, as well as original concoctions, such as the Dark n' Jumpy made with rum, vodka, apricot, and coffee.

Rum and Coke became popular in Cuba soon after Coca-Cola was first exported there in 1900. Strong Water Tavern's version of the Cuba Libre uses barrel-aged cola syrup.

Any liquid odyssey is best anchored by a bite to eat, and the Caribbean-style tapas on the menu are so thoughtfully curated and prepared that you'll want to try several. Cuba, Mexico, Puerto Rico, Colombia, the US Virgin Islands, and the West Indies are all represented by two or three distinctive dishes, and authentic flavors aren't watered down for timid palates. A Jamaican curry features goat and Scotch bonnet peppers, and four different styles of ceviche showcase Florida shrimp (Mexican), snapper (Peruvian), and sea bass (Cuban) or a mix of grouper, shrimp, and scallops (Caribbean). Florida seafood also shines in a Mexican seafood tostada and a Cuban shrimp Creole.

Desserts also have tropical flair, with tastes of coconut, guava, passion fruit, ginger, pineapple, and dulce de leche weaving their way through a sweet selection of cakes, flans, puddings, and more. Or you could just tap your rum captain one last time and end this journey the way you started it: with some rum.

6601 Adventure Way
407-503-5447
loewshotels.com/sapphire-falls-resort/dining/lounges

LAKERIDGE WINERY & VINEYARDS

Florida's largest winery

Grapes are a finicky lot, which is why terroir, the natural environment in which a particular wine is produced, is so important. Factors including the soil, topography, and climate where a grape is grown all affect the flavor of wine. In sunny, sandy Florida, the terroir is most favorable to muscadines, a hardy, thick-skinned, and aromatic sweet grape that many Southerners grew up eating from their own backyard vines.

At Lakeridge Winery & Vineyards, which Gary Cox opened in 1989, the primary line of wines is made from the muscadine grapes that are native to Florida, including red Noble, bronze Carlos, and Welder muscadines. The grapes come from the vineyards on the 127-acre estate, as well as from other contracted vineyards within the Sunshine State.

The heart of the estate is its 35,000-square-foot Spanish-style building, which houses winemaking equipment, a distribution warehouse, a retail wine shop that also sells foods to enjoy in the outdoor picnic area, more than 350,000 gallons of refrigerated stainless-steel storage tanks, and sparkling wine caves that hold more than eighteen thousand bottles. You can learn more about winemaking and the flourishing wine industry in Florida during free forty-five-minute winery tours and tastings offered seven days a week. During the tour, you can enjoy a behind-the-scenes look at winemaking from grape to glass and get a look at the vineyards and

With just five hundred acres under vine, Florida ranks seventh in wine production by state.

Left: Ripe Noble grapes. Photo courtesy of Lakeridge Winery & Vineyards.

Top right: A sampling from the popular Wine and Seafood Festival. Photo courtesy of Lakeridge Winery & Vineyards.

Bottom right: Fun on the stomping line. Photo courtesy of Lakeridge Winery & Vineyards.

production areas before heading to the tasting counter to sample seven varieties of Lakeridge's award-winning wines.

If the forty-five-minute tour leaves you wanting more, visit during one of the winery's monthly family-friendly festivals. Themes vary from chocolate to cheese to seafood, but there's always good food—and plenty of wine—available to enjoy along with live music in the open air. If you really want to get up close and personal, check out the grape stomping during Summerfest in June and at the harvest festival held in July. Whether you prefer your muscadines underfoot or in your glass, there's plenty to experience at Florida's largest winery.

19239 US Hwy. 27 N., Clermont
800-768-WINE
lakeridgewinery.com

THE MEATBALL STOPPE

Meatballs and so much more

You may think you know your meatballs. Maybe you've even gone beyond the holy trinity of beef, pork, and veal and experimented with poultry or veggies on a quest to create the perfect spherical spaghetti staple. But chef Isabella Morgia di Vicari, who owns and operates this homey spot with her husband, Jeff Morgia, really, really knows meatballs. In fact, thirteen distinctly different styles of meatballs are on her menu, made with ingredients ranging from traditional to twist-on-a-classic to downright daring.

Purists will love Nonna's traditional Italian—so did Guy Fieri when he featured the restaurant on *Diners, Drive-Ins and Dives*—as well as the versions inspired by chicken Parmigiana and chicken marsala. There are also mac-and-cheese balls and a vegetarian version that Fieri favored with the house's thick white-bean ragu. All the choices here—including meatballs made with lamb, crab, and even alligator—come with one of seven house-made sauces and are available as a flight, by the bucket, as a "smash" on a fresh ciabatta roll, or with a side of creamy polenta, pasta, or that soulful bean ragu.

Di Vicari is no one-trick pony. She also offers an array of comfort foods from Italy, the Mediterranean, and the United States, as well as vegan and gluten-free options. Her favorite dish is the eggplant stack, "three layers of perfectly breaded and seasoned eggplant slices stacked like a lasagna with three cheeses in between each layer, and topped with our roasted tomato sauce—no marinara sauce in

Spaghetti and meatballs originated in the United States during the first wave of Italian immigration between 1880 and 1920. Meat was more affordable in the United States and quickly become a staple on Italian-American tables.

Top left: "La Famiglia Room" at the Meatball Stoppe. Photo by Eight Fifths.

Top right: A meatball smash. Photo courtesy of the Meatball Stoppe.

Bottom: Chef Isabella Morgia di Vicari. Photo by Eight Fifths.

our house—all prepared to order," she says. She's also partial to the eggplant panino, which is baked with sautéed peppers, onions, and provolone on a ciabatta roll and then topped with arugula, thinly sliced red onions, and the signature pesto mayo.

Her real passion, however, is her customers, and Di Vicari strives to greet them with the warmth typically reserved for family. It is her store's welcoming aroma and environment, Di Vicari maintains, that causes her customers to claim that "it reminds them of their nonna's and mamma's cucina." According to Di Vicari, "This is something that is greatly missing in our world today. When we bring this genuine heartfelt gift to them, what more can we give?"

7325 Lake Underhill Rd.
407-270-6505
themeatballstoppe.com

THE TENNESSEE TRUFFLE

Southern fusion, local ingredients

No, truffles do not abound in the state of Tennessee. The name of this funky little spot on Sanford's historic main drag is chef Nat Russell's affectionate nod to one of the delicacies of his home state: the wild ramps that sprout up in patches in the mountains each spring. Not quite a leek, not quite a scallion, the ramp's bulbs and greens are both treasured by chefs and amateurs alike for their flavor and versatility in a sauté, on the grill, or in the pickling jar.

The same could be said for Russell's versatility. The Culinary Institute of America grad and former executive chef at Café de France in Winter Park is as adept at making the featherlight biscuits that anchor the breakfast and lunch menus as he is preparing the evening's freshly caught local fish to serve with seasonal accoutrements, such as porcini gnocchi, wild mushrooms, corn, arugula puree, and Meyer lemon preserves.

The exposed brick walls are adorned with paintings of Johnny Cash, B. B. King, and other Tennessee notables, and the vibe here is as unstuffy at dinner as it is at breakfast. With the exception of the artisan bread from Olde Hearth Bread Company, every element of every meal—from the pork from Todd Meyer's Farm used in the sausage gravy to the lardons made from Duroc bacon—is cured, ground, pickled, or baked from scratch in the tiny kitchen. Certain staples are a constant—for example, the delicious lunchtime side of

Chef Nat's dessert take on biscuits and gravy features brown-butter ice cream, Grammy's chocolate gravy, and a dash of Telli black pepper.

Left: Chef Nat Russell outside his restaurant. Photo by Jessica McCarty-Carvajal.
Right: One last sprinkle. Photo by Jessica McCarty-Carvajal.

Mimi's Macaroni and Tomato Salad, made silky with just the right amount of bacon grease, but Russell is forever experimenting and wandering over to the dining room to offer a taste of the smoked maple syrup he'll pair with savory French toast or the brown-butter ice cream that will ultimately melt into a milk-chocolate porter float.

A Memphis native, Russell has come to love what Florida has to offer. He works with small producers, such as the five-acre Perezgang Farms in Sanford, and stocks an assortment of Florida craft brews. While he's yet to find any ramps growing wild here, low-key neighborhood restaurants offering cuisine on par with Russell's are as rare as any truffle.

125 W. First St., Sanford
407-942-3977
thetennesseetruffle.com

SHIRAZ MARKET

Persian grocery and grill

At this modest but jam-packed storefront, you'll find all the ingredients for a Persian feast, from preserved lemons and pomegranate molasses to halal meats and imported cheeses. There's freshly baked pita from Jacksonville's renowned Middle Eastern bakery, Village Bread & Bagel; every two weeks, spinach pie, zaatar pie, cheese pie, and Turkish bread come from Tampa Terrace Bakery; and cream pastries and other sweets make the short journey from Saba Bakes in neighboring Winter Springs.

Nas Rajabi, the market's friendly and energetic young owner, will gladly point customers toward newly acquired items that are sure to go quickly, such as green plums or green almonds. He'll also offer insight on how best to enjoy such foodstuffs as pickled shallots ("with everything!") or faloodeh, a sorbet made with rosewater and vermicelli that is often eaten alongside a scoop of pistachio and saffron ice cream called bastani. Of course, Rajabi stocks house-made versions of both.

If you do decide on sweets, however, you'd be wise to take them to go to leave room for the kitchen's fantastic kebabs. (They're available to go, as well, but somehow taste even better when eaten at one of the two tables right in the middle of the shop.) Seasoned chunks of chicken or beef are cooked in the traditional Persian way—on flat metal skewers over an open flame. For the koobideh, chicken or beef

The red berries of the sumac bush are ground to make a spice that gives Persian food a mild lemony flavor. You'll find it on the shelves and on the table at Shiraz Market.

Left: Just a sampling of the spices for sale at Shiraz Market.

Right: Lamb chops over an open flame. Photo courtesy of Shiraz Market.

is finely ground with onion and spices and left to marinate before being formed over skewers and put on the fire. Grilled tomato, a lime wedge, parsley, and onion come on the side with all the kebabs, which are served atop a bed of impossibly fluffy extra-long-grain saffron rice. On weekends the kitchen might offer a special, such as dizi, a lamb and chickpea soup, with hot lavash bread, or zereshk polo, chicken with rice studded with dried barberries.

Shiraz Market was one of the stops on the itinerary when Andrew Zimmern visited Orlando in 2018, but rest assured that you'll get the same warm reception and wonderful food even if you're not filming for the Food Network. Or, as Rajabi says, "We wouldn't feed you something that we wouldn't eat ourselves. We make honest food with huge amounts of my family's passion."

185 S. Ronald Reagan Blvd., Longwood
407-951-8084
facebook.com/internationalfreshmarket

RANGOLI SWEETS

Festive Indian sweets and snacks

A party isn't quite a party without sweets, and Indian sweets pack a party into every oh-so-sugary bite. From the humble gulab jamun—a buffet staple of dumpling-like spheres of fried, milky batter swimming in rose-scented sugar syrup—to the fancier, fudgy squares of barfi that are decorated with edible silver leaf and offered to guests at weddings and other celebrations, Rangoli Sweets manufactures a slew of sweetmeats and namkeen, or savory snacks.

Owner Ram Narayan began his career in Rajasthan and eventually moved to South Delhi, where he became executive chef of the renowned Evergreen Sweet House in 1985. He opened his Winter Springs business in a dollar-store strip mall in 2004, using his own recipes and the techniques he had perfected through decades of experience. The massive kitchen in back takes up most of the real estate here, with customers coming and going from the parking lot to a small area up front, mostly to pick up catering orders. (Rangoli Sweets also has a catering menu with dozens of vegetarian curries, appetizers, and snacks.) The only decoration comes from the shelves and freezer cases stacked with plastic clamshells of the many varieties of snacks for sale, which are also available through other area retailers. The shop also specializes in ornate gift boxes of sweets for special occasions, and receiving one would make the occasion special indeed.

370 E. SR 434, Winter Springs
407-745-0695
rangolisweetsflorida.com

Khoya, which is made from the solids of dried evaporated milk, is the basis for many Indian sweets.

Top: The unassuming exterior of Rangoli Sweets.

Bottom left: Hot mix combines spicy cashews with fried lentils, chick peas, and other savories for a crunchy snack.

Bottom right: Syrupy sweet gulab jamun are available plain or stuffed with a creamy filling.

ORLANDO MEATS

Whole-animal butcher shop featuring local meats

In an era when home cooks have access to a *batterie de cuisine* featuring Instant Pots, sous-vide machines, and other smart tools, it's easy to forget that truly good meals owe much to old-fashioned methods. This irony is not lost on Edgar Massoni, who has owned and operated Orlando Meats since 2013. At this sleek storefront on a hip stretch of Mills 50 surrounded by local bars and small, independent businesses, there's a full-service butcher shop that breaks down whole animals that have been grass fed and raised on pasture not farther than 150 miles away.

Supply permitting, there are typically a number of showstopper items in the case, from dry-aged porterhouse steaks to lamb loin chops, but because this is a nose-to-tail shop, plenty of workaday cuts are also available, such as shanks, sirloin flap, and the excellent house-made sausages, as well as offal, bones, and fat. All these meal starters—and the techniques used to process them—yield dishes that are time honored and tasty as heck using nothing more than a hot pan and patience.

If patience isn't your strong suit, make your way over to the restaurant side of the store and order something from the ever-changing, no-substitutions seasonal menu and let chef Eliot Hillis and his talented team make it for you. You'll always find the popular Medium Rare Burger (yes, that's its proper name) made with grass-fed beef and served on a French roll with garlic aioli, provolone, and a bacon-enhanced XO sauce, as well as katsu sandwiches and a full menu of "not-sandwiches," including clever pasta dishes and salads featuring produce grown by Sugar Top Farms in Clermont.

Left: Whole beef. Courtesy of Orlando Meats.

Top right: Interior. Courtesy of Orlando Meats.

Bottom right: Smoked corned beef and Swiss with sauerkraut and thousand island on rye. Courtesy of Orlando Meats.

The restaurant, which serves three meals a day plus weekend brunch, is the most visible addition to the new and improved location. Massoni forever shuttered the old place during the new store's lengthy renovation and sold meat at the Audubon Park Community Market until the shop's grand opening in November 2017. No matter how often the menu changes, however, the high quality and humane treatment of the animals that provide for so many meals will remain constant, and if you feel the need for a fancy gadget, you can find a list of butcher-approved tools on the store's website.

728 Virginia Dr.
407-598-0700
orlandomeats.com

VALHALLA BAKERY AND VALKYRIE DOUGHNUTS

Vegan-friendly sweet treats

Celine Duvoisin isn't Orlando's only vegan baker, but her sweet treats are the ones most likely to make you laugh out loud, if only your mouth weren't so full. How about a BFD? This special-order colossus that's roughly the size of a pizza is available in a range of flavors, such as Fruity Pebbles and Chocolate Sprankle, to please your precocious inner child. Another impish option is the Holy Sh*t!, a custom-order layer cake topped with Death Bar (peanut butter, Oreos, and candied brownies), Brookie (brownie and cookie), or s'mores (you know what s'mores are). Those who really want to party go for a special order of all three toppings.

Of course there are off-the-rack specials at both sweet spots that Duvoisin owns and operates. Valhalla Bakery, the original brick-and-mortar shop that she opened at Market on South in 2015, offers cookies, cupcakes, cinnamon rolls, and cake slices baked in-house, plus a limited supply of doughnuts delivered daily from Valkyrie Doughnuts. A favorite among Canucks and Yanks alike is the Nanaimo bar—Duvoisin is from Nanaimo, British Columbia—which consists of a dark-chocolate coconut crust filled with custard and topped with still more dark chocolate.

It's a good thing Celine Duvoisin had a fallback career option. "Professional dog snuggling doesn't seem to be an occupation, so we bake instead . . . and snuggle dogs on our own time," she says.

Left: Celine Duvoisin at Valkyrie Doughnuts. Photo by Cat Lemus Photography.
Right: Mini doughnut atop a soft-serve cone. Photo by Cat Lemus Photography.

As the name suggests, Valkyrie Doughnuts is doughnut focused, with coffee from Foxtail and frozen novelties, including DaJen's Irie Cream from DaJen Eats. This second location sprang into being in 2017, when doughnut demand outstripped the Valhalla staff's ability to produce the requisite amount of doughnuts and doughnut nuggets. Duvoisin can relate to the doughnut jones, admitting that "personally, it's *really* hard to not snag a piping-hot, freshly glazed doughnut, but if I start on nugs, I'll take down a hundred-count box on my own."

Customers at the lively little storefront feel much the same way, and Valkyrie's fan base extends beyond the Orlando area to the many visitors who add the shop to their vacation itineraries, and who could blame them? As the ever-grounded Goddess of Gluten herself describes her holey creations, they're "made from scratch, hand cut, and they don't suck."

TRY IT

Valhalla Bakery
2603 E. South St.
407-613-5968
valhallabakery.com

Valkyrie Doughnuts
160-12226 Corporate Blvd.
valkyriedoughnuts.com

DAJEN EATS CAFÉ & CREAMERY

Vegan food with Jamaican flair

As you enter this café right next door to the Eatonville Town Hall, you'll see a quote on the wall from this historic town's most famous resident, Zora Neale Hurston. DaJen Eats has been part of the Eatonville community only since the summer of 2018, when chef/owner Jenn Ross moved her operation a few miles east from the Citgo gas station where she had served her island-influenced, meat-free fare for a year. But in that short time, her sweet storefront has become a hub for those in Eatonville and beyond who crave a soulful sammie, a cup of Jamaican ginger tea, and some food for thought.

Like so many college students, Ross learned to cook from necessity. She came to Central Florida from Jamaica at the age of sixteen; it was never part of her plan to cook for a living, but her passion for food and the humane treatment of "human and non-human animals" took over, she says. She has taken to sharing her enthusiasm with others not just through her menu but also through cooking classes for children and adults, videos on her DaJen Eats YouTube channel, and her Irie Thoughts Radio podcasts on SoundCloud.

Ross and her staff take their irie, or pleasing, vibes seriously. On a sunny day, the lush murals on the walls positively radiate energy, and

> "Mama exhorted her children at every opportunity to 'jump at the sun.' We might not land on the sun, but at least we would get off the ground." From *Dust Tracks on a Road* by Zora Neale Hurston

Left: Chef Jenn Ross. Courtesy of DaJen Eats.
Right: Jerk and crispy fried chick'n with brown-stew cauliflower and Jamaican rice and peas.

both the service and menu are accommodating. Ross even created a whole new dish when she realized that the long lines at her former location moved slowly because so many customers had a tough time choosing between the Buffalo Chick'n and the Jerk Chick'n Sammich. Enter the Identity Crisis Sammich, a happy mashup of both. For bowls, guests can choose toothsome fried or jerk chick'n, sweet-and-spicy or brown-stew cauliflower, or a combo of all the above with Jamaican rice and peas, rainbow broccoli slaw, and grilled pineapple.

As if life here wasn't sweet enough, there are also a dozen or so flavors of the house-made dairy-free ice cream called Irie Cream. Jamaica gets a nod in such flavors as Rum Raisin' the Roof, (Sour) Sop the Madness, and Lime in Da Coconut; Thrilla in Vanilla and Roll Out the Red Velvet Cheesecake will please those who prefer a conservative cone.

Whether you catch Ross on the radio or in her restaurant, you'll soon understand why—and be thankful that she let her passion dictate her path in life.

323 E. Kennedy Blvd.
407-775-5791
dajeneats.com

Home-style Southern fare

John Rivers is best known in Orlando's culinary community for the Texas-inspired 4 Rivers Smokehouse, a labor of love that started with a barbecue fund-raiser back in 2004, led to a brick-and-mortar location in Winter Park in 2009, and now boasts more than a dozen locations all over Florida. For now, however, there is only one place to get the comfort-food classics that Rivers grew up on, and that's the COOP in Winter Park's historic Hannibal Square neighborhood.

Even the block where the COOP roosts is as Southern as can be. Nearby neighbors include the Ideal Women's Club, the Hannibal Square Heritage Center, and the Ward Chapel AME Church, which in 2018 celebrated 125 years of ministry. The COOP is a spring chicken by comparison—the bright red building opened for business on this lively corner in 2014—but it feels like it's been there forever. The bright and open dining room is filled with the kinds of care-worn wooden tables and chairs that a family might accumulate and treasure over time, and the back patio feels like home.

The food feels like home, too, and that's just the way Rivers intended it to be. Rivers was raised in the South and credits his grandmother, a native of Charleston, with teaching him to enjoy down-home flavors and seasonings. Rivers says, "My love for Southern comfort food is as second nature as humid evenings and college football! The menu at the COOP is a reflection of the food I grew up eating."

Breakfast time is a celebration of carbs in all their glory, when classic waffles, pancakes, biscuits, and French toast are served alongside contemporary takes, such as the red-velvet-cake waffle or caramelized-croissant French toast. Eggs from Lake Meadow Naturals appear in a skillet with pulled pork atop a chicken-and-

Top left: Croissant French toast. Photo courtesy of the COOP.

Bottom left: Shrimp and grits, fried chicken, and Southern sides. Photo courtesy of the COOP.

Right: Fried chicken is just as good on the go. Photo courtesy of the COOP.

waffle Benedict and on a plate of cormeal-crusted catfish and Anson Mills grits. Crunchy, peppery fried chicken is a favorite during lunch and dinner, along with Southern staples such as meatloaf and chicken fried steak, and the bevy of sides will make any Southerner's heart go pitty-pat.

Both the provenance and the portion sizes of the dishes here are decidedly and delightfully old school, but should there be room for dessert, there's also a sweet selection of moon pies, hand pies, cake slices, banana pudding, and more. True Southern hospitality forbids letting a guest walk away hungry, and hospitality abounds here.

610 W. Morse Blvd., Winter Park
407-843-2667
asouthernaffair.com

KRUNGTHEP TEA TIME (page 160)

P IS FOR PIE BAKE SHOP (page 198)

ORLANDO MEATS (page 76)

1921 MOUNT DORA (page 4)

PLANT STREET MARKET (page 158)

STRONG WATER TAVERN (page 64)

THE BOHEME (page 188)

JIMOTTI'S RESTAURANT (page 176)

ART SMITH'S HOMECOMIN' AT DISNEY SPRINGS (page 102)

THE WHISKEY (page 130)

TASTE OF CHENGDU (page 104)

STICKY RICE LAO STREET FOOD (page 182)

CHEF WANG'S KITCHEN (page 114)

THE RUSTY SPOON (page 34)

LITTLE VIETNAM (page 120)

GAPA (page 192)

DISNEY SPRINGS

Menu magic, multiple eateries

There's so much to do, see, and buy at Disney Springs—Disney's open-air oasis for shopping, dining, and entertainment—that it may be tempting to slot mealtime as just another item on the day's to-do list. Don't.

With more than sixty eateries, from kiosks to rooftops, and chefs whose names you may have seen on a hotel restaurant in Vegas, a list of James Beard Award winners, or both, the wealth of choices can seem daunting. Take a deep breath and a second look at the handful of excellent options that were born and raised in Florida.

The Polite Pig, the more casual but still mannerly younger sibling of the Ravenous Pig in Winter Park, offers an array of barbecue, salads, and sides with Sunshine State style. Chef/owners James and Julie Petrakis bring the same commitment to quality ingredients, scratch cooking, and playful, flavorful plates that they do to their more upscale digs several miles north. Little details matter here, as with the fennel-apple slaw served on a pulled-pork sandwich or the avocado-chipotle dressing and roasted corn on the cob salad. Beer matters, too, and theirs is from their own Cask & Larder Brewery as well as other Central Florida breweries, such as Red Cypress Brewery and Central 28 Beer Company.

Master Sommelier George Miliotes offers more than 130 wines at Wine Bar George and has trained his staff to help you navigate these hand-selected offerings to enjoy as a flight, paired with a small plate, alongside a cheese and charcuterie board, or with a

> Anyone who lived in Orlando in the mid-1970s or '80s will remember Disney's original vision for this area: Lake Buena Vista Shopping Village.

Left: Cheese and charcuterie board. Photo courtesy of Wine Bar George.
Right: Moonshine flight. Photo courtesy of Chef Art Smith's Homecomin'.

family-style plate of wine-braised chicken, skirt steak, or whole grilled sea bass. Some of the most precious (read, pricey) pours are available by the ounce so that you can splurge as much or as little as you like.

Chef and author Art Smith has worked for two Florida governors as well as Oprah, and while he's behind successful restaurants in Chicago, Atlanta, and other out-of-state locales, Florida is where his home and heart remain. At Chef Art Smith's Homecomin', comfort reigns in such dishes as buttermilk-brined fried chicken and the Capitol Meatloaf he often made during his time at the Governor's Mansion. Florida seafood takes a star turn on the Big Fish Sandwich, in a Key West shrimp cocktail, and as a grilled grouper entrée served with creamed kale and collards.

For tacos, burritos, and bowls on the fly, the 4 Rivers Cantina Barbacoa Food Truck offers 4 Rivers's famous barbecue with a Mexican twist. If you can't decide whether to fill your taco cone with brisket barbacoa or pork sofrito, fret not—you can always come back to Disney Springs.

1486 E. Buena Vista Dr.
disneysprings.com

Capital cuisine from Sichuan

When non-Chinese people discuss or devour Sichuan dishes, spicy ones get all the attention. To be sure, the dried chilies added to many dishes and the pink Sichuan peppercorns used for making the cuisine's tongue-numbing chili oil are nothing if not assertive, and the one or two Sichuan items on the menu at a Cantonese restaurant might stand apart from the Americanized others only because of their extreme heat. But Chinese cooking in general relies on a spectrum of flavors—including salty, sour, sweet, pungent, and bitter—and Sichuan cooks combine these elements to make flavors that are distinct but hard to define. At his humble yet welcoming restaurant attached to a Best Western between Parramore and Pine Hills, chef Xiong "Tiger" Tang takes every element, flavor-wise and otherwise, into account.

A golden lucky cat near the cash register greets guests with a perpetual wave, but that's the lone bit of kitsch on display here. The Sichuan province is known for its agricultural riches, and the only pops of color in the spare but warm dining room are from garlands of papier-mâché chilies, green bell peppers, and other vegetables. Large color posters superimposed with Chinese calligraphy show photo collages of the spices used in the Sichuan province where Tang, a native of the capital, Chengdu, went to cooking school.

Meals begin with small, cold dishes, some spicy and some not, of cucumbers or eggplant, rabbit or pork. There's also a dish featuring

Traditional Sichuan "fish-fragrant" sauce is made with light and dark soy sauces, rice wine, fermented bean paste, and other ingredients, but no fish or seafood of any kind.

Left: A cold starter of black fungus with peanuts.

Center: Sichuan-flavored pork dumplings.

Right: Shrimp with ground pork and fresh green peppers.

black fungus and peanuts showcasing a mix of textures. Soups, dumplings, and wontons are other traditional ways to kick off a meal. From there diners can choose from an array of noodle dishes, hot pots, and dry-fried dishes ranging from the familiar (mapo tofu) to the exotic (spicy and sour pig intestine soup). There's also cumin lamb, double-fried pork belly, and vegetarian-friendly dishes.

Tang speaks fondly of the village restaurants in his home province—homey places that have been around for generations and thrive by focusing on one cuisine and doing it well. Taste of Chengdu opened its doors in the fall of 2018, making it a relative newcomer in a neighborhood long known for good, if quirky, and reasonably priced food finds. But if the critical acclaim and groups of friends and colleagues waiting to get inside the minute the restaurant opens for lunch are any indication, Tang might well find himself running the kind of restaurant that he so loved back home.

2030 W. Colonial Dr.
407-839-1983
facebook.com/tasteofchengdu

Iranian, Middle Eastern, and French pastries and bread

It's a suburban cliché that the best food can be found in a random strip mall, especially in Central Florida, where so many random strip malls (and so much good food) abound. A less common trope, however, is a third-generation baker from Tehran operating a small but successful business in the back end of a commerce center behind a batting cage and surrounded by auto-glass repair and truck-accessory stores. But that's exactly where you'll find Mohsen Tehrani, and on Fridays and Saturdays when the hot barbari bread comes out of the oven, that's where you'll find his regular customers too.

Thicker than most flatbreads, barbari bread is a long, ridged oblong loaf sprinkled with white sesame and black kalonji (also known as Nigella) seeds. Here the chewy loaves are made from hard spring wheat and as long as an adult's arm. Families chat in Farsi while they help themselves to free cups of self-serve coffee and load up on a week's worth of bread and possibly a sweet treat for the ride home. By some act of serendipity, the customers trickle in steadily but slowly; there isn't room for more than four or five souls in the tiny area in front of the pastry-packed case.

There's plenty of room to linger, however, at the newer Saba Bakes outpost inside the International Food Club, the massive global grocery store about twenty miles southwest. Open since the fall of 2018, the bakery sells all its products here with room to sit and enjoy on-site. Look for Iranian specialties such as crumbly, clover-shaped chickpea cookies; Zaban, a puff pastry that looks like a

Left: A fresh loaf of barbari bread.

Right: Cream pastries are available by the pound.

cross between a doughnut and a ladyfinger; French cream pastries flavored with chocolate and coffee and sold by the pound; syrupy zulbia, the Persian version of Indian jalebi, which looks similar to funnel cake; bamieh, saffron, and rosewater doughnuts the size of hush puppies; and sheets of hard, cracker-like golden sweet bread made with yogurt, saffron, and cardamom.

For now, the original bakery, which Tehrani opened after years of baking for family and friends, is the only place to get these specialties hot from the oven. In lieu of a Krispy Kreme–style "Hot Now" sign, regulars check the store's Facebook page to find out when certain specialties are available fresh. Whatever the weekend's specialty might be, the conversation and the free coffee will surely be flowing.

1255 Belle Ave. #172, Winter Springs
407-799-7225
sababakes.com

Corn, cucumbers, and a country café and market

Say the word "Zellwood" to people who grew up in Central Florida and their thoughts will immediately turn not to the one-stoplight town thirty miles west of Orlando but to ears of sweet corn. For nearly forty years, the annual Zellwood Corn Festival welcomed Floridians from all over to this open-air party featuring live music, corn-themed crafts, and thousands of ears of corn. The last Zellwood Corn Festival was held in 2013, but there's still sweet corn to enjoy. If it didn't come from Long & Scott Farms, however, it's simply not Zellwood corn.

Established in 1963 by Frank Scott Jr. and his friend Billy Long, the farm is now run by Frank's son Hank along with his son, Sonny. Theirs is the last farm remaining in Zellwood, and in 2001 they trademarked the name Scott's Zellwood Triple-Sweet Gourmet Corn. The sweet bicolor corn is available by the ear, bag, or bushel right on the farm at Scott's Country Market during two growing seasons: from late April to mid-June and again from mid-September through November.

Corn season dovetails with the season for the farm's other main crop, Kirby cucumbers. These smaller, thinner-skinned cukes are delicious fresh but also ideal for pickling—the next time you open a jar of pickles from the grocery store, they might have been grown here.

There's plenty of fresh produce for sale in the market even when corn and cucumbers aren't in season. The farm grows organic

> A popular sight at the Zellwood Corn Festival was Big Bertha, a 350-gallon boiler that cooked 1,650 ears of corn every nine minutes.

Left: Cabbages and strawberries grown at Long & Scott Farms.
Right: Hank Scott with Rebecca Scott Tyndall. Photo by AaronVan.

strawberries in the winter, along with sweet onions, kale, collards, mustard greens, and more than 450 acres of green, red, and savoy cabbage. Spring and fall might bring yellow squash, zucchini, okra, and conch peas, a shelling pea prized for its delicate texture and flavor.

At Scott's Country Café, you can enjoy a bowl of creamy Zellwood sweet corn chowder, thick with yellow and white kernels of corn grown within eyeshot of where you're eating. Dill-pickle soup—a thick soup made with potatoes, carrots, sour cream, and (yep) dill pickles—is a newer addition to the café's menu of breakfast, pulled pork, and chicken-salad sandwiches.

Each fall the farm hosts Scott's Maze Adventures, run by Hank's sister, Rebecca Scott Tyndall. The six-acre maze takes a different shape each year, and families come every weekend to get lost, ride the super slide, or take a ride around the farm on the Sweet Corn Express.

26216 CR 448A, Mount Dora
352-383-6900
longandscottfarms.com

COFFEE FOR A CAUSE

Caffeine and community

There's just something about a good cup of coffee that inspires conversation and builds community, and with literally dozens of coffee roasters setting up shop in Central Florida since the late aughts, you can even forge that caffeinated bond over locally roasted joe. A few purveyors, though, have taken the concept of community several steps further and modeled their businesses to give back and make change, both in Orlando and beyond.

Downtown CREDO purchases its beans directly from growers and roasts the beans in small batches in partnership with Coffee Roasters Alliance. The profits from all three of its pay-what-you-wish locations fund projects to benefit children, promote Orlando city parks, and support authentic, diverse local communities.

The volunteer staffers at Palate Coffee Brewery aren't just pouring coffee. They're pouring all their profits into Love Missions, which is dedicated to abolishing human trafficking.

Axum Coffee is named for the city in Ethiopia that has received all its profits since the first location opened in 2005. Axum also operates the food and beverage side of Orlando Cat Café, where guests enjoy the sight of a dozen or so adoptable cats roaming freely in the one-thousand-square-foot play area. In exchange for a reservation and a small entry fee, guests can take their lattes to the other side of the window and get to know the furry residents up close and personal.

TRY IT

Axum Coffee
146 W. Plant St., Winter Garden
426 W. Plant St., Winter Garden
2000 Fowler Grove Blvd., Winter Garden
axumcoffee.com

Left: Axum Coffee at Plant Street Market. Photo courtesy of the City of Winter Garden.

Right: Coffee is for people, not cats. Photo courtesy of Orlando Cat Café.

Orlando Cat Café
532 Cagan Park Ave., Clermont
352-989-4820
orlandocatcafe.com

Downtown CREDO
706 W. Smith St.
550 E. Rollins St.
885 N. Orange Ave.
407-519-0643
downtowncredo.com

Palate Coffee Brewery
105 W. Second St., Sanford
321-363-0661
sanfordcoffee.com

Puff pride

As artisan food trends go, marshmallows have a way to go before they can boast the same ubiquity as cupcakes or doughnuts, but perhaps their slower rise to fame—and longer shelf life—will equal more staying power. In fact, this comforting confection is the sweet foundation for not one but two thriving businesses for two Central Florida couples.

Julie Summers fell in love with marshmallows when she was a little girl while visiting a factory in Las Vegas. The marshmallows that she crafts with her wife, Jean, are about as far from factory made as can be. Every treat that Sugar Rush Marshmallows offers is made from scratch, including the extracts, and cut, sorted, and bagged by hand. Flavors from cold-brew coffee to churro are available by the bag through mail order as well as at pop-ups and food truck rallies. Customers there clamor for s'mores with handmade graham crackers and Ghirardelli chocolate; frozen s'mores stuffed with a nugget of graham cracker–dusted, scratch-made ice cream; and shortcake-style desserts with fluffy marshmallow batter.

Wondermade cofounder Nathan Clark may not have had a lifelong love affair with marshmallows, but he sure took to them fast. Not long after gifting his wife, Jenn, with a candy thermometer and a marshmallow recipe for Christmas in 2011, the Clarks began selling their creations by mail order all over the world. In 2014 they opened a café in historic downtown Sanford selling a rotating selection of the more than one hundred flavors (all free of preservatives and artificial colors and flavorings) they've made over the years, including key lime pie, birthday cake, and beer. There's also handcrafted ice cream by the scoop in flavors both classic

Rainbow marshmallows are a popular pick. Photo courtesy of Sugar Rush Marshmallows.

(cookies and cream) and contemporary (maple bacon, cornbread, avocado). You might even see one (or all) of the Clarks' six kiddos in the store folding marshmallow boxes or just adding extra cuteness to the store, where it says "Love & Marshmallows" right on the front window.

TRY IT

Sugar Rush Marshmallows
407-988-5406
sugarrushmarshmallows.com

Wondermade Café
214 E. First St., Sanford
407-205-9569
wondermade.com

Noodles and other dishes from northern China

Northern Chinese cuisine is known for hand-pulled noodles, and Beijing native Jian Hua Wang exhibits a masterful hand with them at his Chinatown Plaza restaurant. When Chef Wang's Kitchen opened for business in the spring of 2018, a spirited social media debate ensued as to whether or not his version of beef chow fun was the best in town. City officials have yet to bestow that honor on any chef, and while Wang's noodle dishes—also worth fighting over—from other parts of China.

Thin slices of soy-braised beef shank are served as a cold starter, as is bone-in Sichuan-style chicken in a bowl of fiery chili oil with peanuts and sesame. Dry-pot cooking combines the same spicy elements of hot-pot cooking but without the broth. Here, cauliflower with bits of tofu and green pepper gets increasingly more intense as it bubbles in a small wok on the table.

Wang's northern roots come through sharable dishes, such as a Beijing pork pancake, chive pockets, and delicate dumplings filled with pork and Napa cabbage. Wang's version of zha jiang mian, a dish that often contains pork, features a sauce made of three different fermented bean pastes over tender wheat noodles with green soybeans and slivers of cucumber and scallion.

5148 W. Colonial Dr.
407-930-3188

Zha jiang mian is a classic dish from northern China. The name translates to "fried sauce noodles."

Top left: Dry pot cooked cauliflower. Photo by AaronVan.

Top right: Zha jiang mian is a dish from Beijing. Photo by AaronVan.

Bottom: The dining room at Chef Wang's Kitchen. Photo by AaronVan.

1ST ORIENTAL MARKET

Orlando's largest Asian grocery store

You could easily spend an entire day on a progressive dine at the restaurants in Chinatown Plaza. The run-down shopping center that serves many of Orlando's Asian communities is home to several excellent small restaurants serving tastes of Vietnam (Pho Viet), Korea (BBB Tofu House), China (Chef Wang's Kitchen), and Japan (Sapporo Ramen). Like so many suburban plazas filled with nail salons and Sprint stores, however, the anchor here is the supermarket. At this one, Asian families shop for their day-to-day needs, and culinary tourists scour the aisles for interesting and unfamiliar finds.

Small stalls near the store's entrance sell baked goods and boba tea, but the biggest draw for prepared foods is inside and around the corner. Whole salted chickens, Peking-style ducks, and sides of roasted pork hang in a window waiting for the man behind the counter to break them down with a cleaver upon order. When your parcel of protein is safely secured in Styrofoam, you're free to explore the rest of the store for fresh produce, live seafood, and every conceivable part of the pig, as well as frozen and nonperishable specialties from all over Asia.

5132 W. Colonial Dr.
407-292-3668
1storiental.com

A young shopper with Japanese whistle candies. Photo by AaronVan.

Cuban café

Black Bean Deli has been a neighborhood favorite for empanadas, sandwiches, and other grab-and-go Cuban fare since Andres Corton opened the original location in Winter Park in 2002. Seating there was (and is) limited to an outdoor table and a stool or two near the queue for the window, so in 2013 when Corton expanded his Cuban comfort-food fiefdom to a larger location on Colonial Drive, BBD fans rejoiced.

The outdoor patio offers plenty of room to relax and enjoy a café con leche, a kombucha, or a glass of wine along with plates of Spanish baked chicken or the ground beef stew with raisins and olives called picadillo; weekly specials include Havana pork and ropa vieja, a classic dish made with shredded steak that translates to "old clothes." Weekday breakfast is a limited but leisurely affair once the morning rush is over and light pours in through the huge plate-glass windows that give an architectural hint to the midcentury building's original incarnation: gas station. More recently it was home to another well-loved Cuban restaurant, Vega's Café, where between 1976 and 2012 generations of guests came to enjoy Cuban sandwiches and black-bean soup.

You can still enjoy those items here—it's called Black Bean Deli for a reason—though the decor and presentation of the traditional dishes that are served all share a spiffed-up minimalist

Historians disagree on the origins of the Elena Ruz sandwich—some stories claim its namesake was a 1920s-era socialite from Havana—but most agree on its composition: turkey, cream cheese, and strawberry jam on eggy medianoche bread. Look for it on BBD's breakfast menu.

Left: Outside Black Bean Deli. Photo by AaronVan.

Right: Cuban coffee and a ham, egg, and cheese sandwich on the patio. Photo by AaronVan.

vibe that makes it a perfect fit with its Mills 50 neighbors. The only ornamental touches in the clean white space outfitted with bamboo bistro chairs and sleek blond-wood banquettes are a few potted plants, a letter board, and a display of the many "best of" awards that BBD has racked up.

Another BBD outlet has served guests at the Amway Center since 2014, and future plans include a new location at another now-shuttered iconic Central Florida spot, the former Winnie's Oriental Garden restaurant in Winter Park. (Once it opens, the other Winter Park location will become the full-time outlet for BBD's catering operation.) Don't expect Chino-Latino menu items at this new space—it'll have the same menu and look as its siblings—but do expect authentic flavors, generous portions, and gracious service. It's the Black Bean Deli way of doing things.

1835 E. Colonial Dr.
407-203-0922

325 S. Orlando Ave., Winter Park
407-628-0294

1346 N. Orange Ave., Winter Park (coming 2019)

blackbeandeli.com

Culture, cuisine, and commerce in Mills 50

The Mills 50 district—the blocks surrounding the intersection of Mills Avenue and Highway 50 (Colonial Drive)—is one of Orlando's several official Main Street Districts that bring together small businesses, artists, and residents to enhance and preserve each neighborhood's distinct character. The districts were established in 2008, but decades before the official rebrand locals were flocking to the area then known as Little Vietnam to shop for Asian gifts and groceries and to enjoy a bowl of pho during what was often their first foray into Vietnamese cuisine.

The first refugees from Vietnam came to the area in the 1970s, and Orange County is still home to the largest Asian population in the state. These new residents opened restaurants, markets, and more throughout the 1980s and '90s, and longtime residents soon came to explore. Many of the area's most iconic Vietnamese businesses are still thriving today; some, such as Pho 88, are now run by the original owners' grown children.

The area will seem familiar to anyone who has wandered through an Asian enclave in a major American city, but there are certain aspects to Orlando's Little Vietnam that are pure Florida. The bright, pastel-heavy color palette—adorning the original buildings themselves and the murals painted on them by local artists throughout the 2010s—seems to hum under the city's nearly always present sunshine. Midcentury architecture, cinderblock, and stucco add to the mix, as do the myriad places to get an excellent meal along with a history lesson.

Left: Tien Hung Market sells groceries from all over Asia. Photo by AaronVan.

Right: Mural by Andrew Spear on Little Saigon building. Photo by AaronVan.

TRY IT

Dong A Supermarket is a favorite spot for local chefs in
search of Asian ingredients.
812-816 Mills Ave., 407-898-9227
dongacorporation.com

Little Saigon Restaurant is one of the oldest eateries in the area.
1106 E. Colonial Dr., 407-423-8539
littlesaigonrestaurant.com

Pho 88 Vietnamese Restaurant is one of the busier spots around,
offering a full menu of pho, rice dishes, stir-fries, and salads.
730 N. Mills Ave., 407-897-3488
pho88orlando.com

Vietnam Cuisine is one of the tiniest but tastiest restaurants on the block.
1224 E. Colonial Dr., 407-228-7053

Anh Hong Restaurant is a casual corner spot that consistently
racks up honors from local media.
1124 E. Colonial Dr., 407-999-2656
anhhongorlando.com

Tien Hung Market Oriental Food Center offers a wide range of
groceries as well as bagged kits for making banh mi.
1110 E. Colonial Dr., 407-422-0067
facebook.com/Tien-Hung-Market-Oriental-Food-Center-134235386622586

Contemporary cuisine in an opulent setting

On the second floor of Disney's eight-hundred-room Grand Floridian Resort and Spa is a hushed and opulent restaurant that welcomes a mere fifty guests each evening. Those fortunate few—who may have reserved their table up to six months in advance—enjoy seven or ten courses prepared by chef Aimée Rivera and her culinary team, a wine list with more than seven hundred bottles from thirty-five different regions, and attentive service from a waitstaff that dedicates two servers to each table in order to deliver a seamless dining experience.

The resort and its gracious grounds are modeled after Florida's seaside resorts during the Victorian era, and each evening the Grand Floridian Society Orchestra entertains guests with live jazz and ragtime in the lobby. It's much quieter upstairs, where the interior of Victoria & Albert's would likely have impressed the royal couple. Gold, cream, and crimson shimmer in the warm lighting, and the most notable sounds are of the harpist plucking out a tune or the sighs of guests enjoying an amuse-bouche, a spoonful of caviar, or chocolates made by the resident chocolatier.

Those who desire an even more personalized experience can book a table in Queen Victoria's Room, which accommodates just eight guests each evening for ten courses with exclusive wine pairings,

> Sometimes little things make a big impression. Here, those things include an upholstered footstool for each lady to rest her purse, the wooden box custom-made to house and present a selection of chocolates, and the personalized menu that each guest takes home as a souvenir.

Left: Lamb loin with rainbow carrots and banana curry. Photo courtesy of Walt Disney World.
Right: The cheese cart at Victoria & Albert's. Photo courtesy of Walt Disney World.

French trolley service, and tableside preparation. The Chef's Table in the grand kitchen seats ten guests for a ten-course meal that kicks off with a champagne toast with the chef and offers a full view of the kitchen's constant, focused action.

No matter which experience you select, expect to dine for at least three hours (more if you choose to add a caviar course). All menus begin with an amuse-bouche and offer different breads and butters between courses. The evening ends with the cheese trolley, an assortment of desserts and coffee and tea service with friandises. In between, expect refined flavors and the finest ingredients from all over the world in such dishes as lobster with Zellwood corn and Espelette pepper or wild Texas boar dusted with onion ash. With cuisine, service, and ambience at this level of excellence and opulence, it's easy to understand why Victoria & Albert's is Orlando's only restaurant that has been granted AAA Five-Diamond status.

Disney's Grand Floridian Resort and Spa
4401 Floridian Way
407-939-3862
victoria-alberts.com

WINTER GARDEN FARMERS MARKET

America's favorite farmers market

No one in Winter Garden was especially surprised in 2018 when the Winter Garden Farmers Market was voted the number one farmers' market in the United States by American Farmland Trust. After all, the trust had granted the market the same distinction the year before, and the year before that as well. And what's not to love? The self-professed "hometown market" is under the open-air pavilion smack-dab in the middle of what is arguably Orange County's homiest hometown. Historic Winter Garden is pet friendly, bike friendly, and pedestrian friendly, and on Saturdays it's farmer friendly too.

The market's primary focus is on produce, plants, and specialty food, and you'll find a huge selection of each on sale from local vendors. Look for organic produce from Frog Song Organics, Orlando-made almond milk from SwellMilk, natural fruit spreads from Melatta, espresso and cold brew from Piccolo Coffee Co., and Sicilian-style chocolate handmade by Cocoa Brothers.

300 W. Plant St., Winter Garden
wintergardenfarmersmarket.com

The twenty-two-mile West Orange Trail is a favorite among cyclists and joggers and runs right through the middle of downtown Winter Garden.

Top: Strolling the farmers' market. Photo courtesy of the City of Winter Garden.

Bottom: Fresh market produce. Photo courtesy of the City of Winter Garden.

CENTRAL FLORIDA ALE TRAIL

Local craft beer journey

There's a pot (or rather a growler) full of gold (or possibly amber) at the end of the Central Florida Ale Trail, and starting the journey couldn't be easier—just visit one of the craft breweries on the trail and ask for your free map. Then visit each brewery on the list to get your map stamped, turn in the completed map on your last stop, and receive a free growler of beer. Simple!

Fortunately, there's no time limit imposed on this trek because there are twenty-five breweries and counting on a trail that spans four counties. The bulk of the dots on the map are in Orlando, from Orlando Brewing, Orlando's original organic brewer, to young upstarts such as Dead Lizard Brewing and Orange County Brewers.

In Lake County, Eustis-based Wolf Branch Brewing Co. offers Belgian-style dubbels, tripels, saisons, and witbiers; you'll need to voyage to Volusia County to sample the El Bulli Imperial Milk Stout or Groveland Road Blood Orange IPA at Central 28 Beer Company in DeBary or the Daytona Dirty Blonde at Persimmon Hollow Brewing Co. in DeLand.

Seminole County is fast becoming a tour in itself, with Sanford's historic district alone boasting five breweries within walking distance of one another. Two of them—Wop's Hops Brewing

Redlight Redlight, which opened a craft beer bar in Winter Park in 2005 and now calls Audubon Park home, has twenty-four draft handles, two hand-pumped beer engines, and more than three hundred bottled beers. It began brewing in-house in 2014.

Left: Red Cypress Brewery head brewer Garrett Ward (right) with taproom manager Chris Belcher. Photo by Amy Drew Thompson.

Right: Have map will travel. Photo by Amy Drew Thompson.

Company and Sanford Brewing Company—have kitchens and full menus so you can pair your Hail Caesar blonde ale with a house-made meatball sandwich (Wop's) or your Top Hat ESB with mac and cheese (Sanford Brewing).

There's no kitchen at Hourglass Brewing in Longwood because it doesn't need one. Customers can walk next door to Wako Taco, order burritos, nachos, or tacos, and wait for delivery on the brewery's side. Ditto Crooked Can Brewing Company, whose taproom is inside Winter Garden's bustling Plant Street Market and which welcomes guests to enjoy their sushi, wood-fired pizza, or other take-out items purchased from the market's vendors along with a pint or a flight inside or on the patio. Winter Park's Cask & Larder is a notable exception to the restaurant-adjacent brewery model; its small-batch brews are produced inside the Ravenous Pig, a full-service, sit-down restaurant featuring locally sourced seasonal fare.

Start your journey wherever you like, but do start it soon and, for heaven's sake, pace yourself—there are an awful lot of pints on the road to growler glory. It's a good thing they're filled with some of the finest and most imaginative brews in the state.

centralfloridaaletrail.com

Neapolitan pizza joint

If you want one of chef/owner Bruno Zacchini's beautifully blistered Neopolitan pies, you're just going to have to wait. Not for the pizza itself—each one cooks in a mere ninety seconds in the thousand-degree wood-fired oven—but do prepare to sit a spell before you score a table because this joint has been a hit since it first opened its doors in the Hourglass District in the summer of 2016. If waiting isn't your thing, use Uber Eats, or place an online order two days in advance and pick up a pizza party to go for you and a dozen friends. Don't think about calling, though, because there is no phone on the premises.

The lack of a jangling landline allows the staff to do what it does best, and that's making and serving twelve-inch pizzas made from a simple cold-fermented dough and topped with creative combos of the freshest ingredients. Like a good wine list, the menu features a handful of carefully curated "reds" and "whites." Reds range from the classic margherita with basil, fresh mozzarella, pecorino cheese, and extra-virgin olive oil to the Crimson Ghost with Calabrian chilies, spicy soppressata, fresh mozzarella, basil, and hot honey. On the white side, the Dude is a simple standout with just three cheeses— fresh mozzarella, pecorino, and taleggio—and lots of freshly ground black pepper. Cheese-free pies are vegan friendly and flavorful.

The kiln-dried red oak that fuels the oven also lends flavor to starters of wine-braised octopus or cauliflower with a sweet and sour

Pizzas often nod to pop culture, such as the Burt Reynolds-inspired special the Bandit, with smoked mozzarella, scallion cream, fresh corn, guanciale, and pickled red onion.

Left: Pizza blanco. Photo courtesy of Pizza Bruno.

Right: Stracciatella with strawberries, pistachios, mint, and balsamic. Photo courtesy of Pizza Bruno.

sauce made with chile peppers and golden raisins. During weekend brunch, Zacchini fires up Dutch baby pancakes and calzones and serves the house's incredible meatballs over polenta.

While there's no official Florida style of pizza just yet, Zacchini's version may just win your vote. The Florida native is as passionate about ingredients from his home state as he is about combining them to make the perfect pie. Look for locally sourced Italian sausage, rock shrimp, heirloom tomatoes, and micro-basil on the menu and on the specials board. You'll have plenty of time to peruse them both while you wait, but it's a laid-back enough spot for lingering with a can of Lambrusco or a local craft beer. Enjoy watching the tables full of families and twenty-somethings alike ooh and aah as they divvy up slices, knowing you'll be doing the same very soon.

3990 Curry Ford Rd.
pizzabrunofl.com

THE WHISKEY

Burgers and booze

More than two dozen restaurants can be found on the mile-and-a-half stretch of Sand Lake Road known as Restaurant Row, and some of them even serve burgers. It's also a safe bet that you'll be able to find a bar offering a decent selection of whiskey, but if you're looking for all of the above in low-key but lively environs, then your search should end here.

More than eighty whiskeys are available as regular or tasting-sized pours at prices that will appeal to both neophytes and connoisseurs. There's an equally impressive selection of rye, bourbon, and scotch, and the restaurant hosts regular tasting events to educate fans about the nuances of its vast and varied offerings. The burgers are a two-fisted lot, with layers of flavor in each chef-selected topping. The Salty Pear is paired with bourbon bacon, brie, whiskey onions, and a bourbon-poached pear, and the pimiento cheese–slathered Southerner gets its crunch from a fried green tomato.

7563 W. Sand Lake Rd.
407-930-6517
downatthewhiskey.com

The Salty Pear. Photo by AaronVan.

Mexican food with a side of art

From the murals on the walls to the books for sale in the lobby to the dishes on the menu, this casual restaurant is filled with stories. Co-owner Joseph Creech's story began in Mexico, where he was born and lived until the age of six, when his missionary parents moved back to Central Florida. Over the years, he and his younger brother, co-owner David, both did missionary work in Mexico and fell in love with the food and culture. Joseph also fell in love with Mexico City native Seydi Plata, who moved to Florida and married Joseph in 2005.

The tacos, tostadas, sides, and soups, which guests order inside and then enjoy on the covered outdoor patio, are inspired by dishes from Mexico's street vendors as well as generations-old recipes from Seydi's family. It's not uncommon to hear a guest exclaim that the flan is "just like my mother's," which is just the kind of praise that the Creeches treasure. Their classic version is impossibly dense and creamy, with the perfect amount of char in the caramel sauce. The chocolate version, or xocoflan, includes a layer of chocolate cake baked underneath a layer of flan de queso.

Guests can draw inspiration not just from a suadero taco made from seared brisket—the kind Seydi craved when she left Mexico—or a soulful bowl of marrow and mushroom soup but also from the beautiful surroundings. Artists from Lapiztola, a collective based in Oaxaca, created the murals that line the lobby and the building's exterior. Just like the other works in the collective's canon, the

> The restaurant's stated mission is "to highlight and celebrate Mexican food, culture, and art by providing authentic Mexican flavors loaded with originality."

Left: Lunch and beer. Courtesy of Hunger Street Tacos.

Right: Xocoflan. Courtesy of Hunger Street Tacos.

murals highlight the social and political injustices that cause strife in their country. Motorists along busy Fairbanks Avenue get a glimpse of *La Palabra Florece*, which translates to "the word flourishes." It is the artists' response to the forceful removal of a mural of theirs in Oaxaca that paid tribute to a slain human rights activist.

Collaborating with creative talent just seems to come naturally to Team Hunger Street, as it does during pop-ups at nearby venues such as The Heavy. One such experience is called Cuate, a name that comes from the Nahuatl word "cōātl," meaning close friend. With just ten guests per seating, this Mexican tasting menu experience is meant to be shared with others. Given the intimate nature of the meal and the time required to truly savor each creative course, you're sure to leave with friendly feelings toward everyone involved.

2103 W. Fairbanks Ave., Winter Park

321-444-6270

hungerstreettacos.com

REEL FISH COASTAL KITCHEN + BAR

Full-service Southern seafood

The rustic fish camp vibe that this Winter Park restaurant claims to embody isn't immediately obvious—it's doubtful that the Depression-era workers along Florida's riverbanks ever dined on avocado toast or chilaquiles—yet the kitchen's commitment to local Florida seafood is genuine.

Mayport shrimp are caught off the coast near Jacksonville, fried, and served with fries and hush puppies on the "Fish Camp Classic" section of the menu. Ports all over the state yield the fresh snapper, grouper, hogfish, and swordfish that appear in daily chalkboard specials or, with the exception of the swordfish, as owner Fred Thimm's favorite dish, the whole fish. Sold by the pound, the day's catch is battered and fried or roasted in the oven and then served with fries and a very Southern side of smothered tomatoes and okra.

Sometimes commitment to a theme can veer too far overboard; fish camps in the 1930s sold little more than iced tea to drink. Luckily, the wine list here is completely contemporary, something you'll be grateful for as you sip a sparkling French rosé.

1234 N. Orange Ave., Winter Park
407-543-3474
reelfishcoastal.com

"One of the nicest things about owning a seafood restaurant in Florida is that I meet a lot of people who know more about seafood than I do, so I never try to BS anyone."
– Fred Thimm

Top left: Oysters on the half shell. Courtesy of Reel Fish Coastal Kitchen + Bar.

Top right: Shrimp po' boy. Courtesy of Reel Fish Coastal Kitchen + Bar.

Bottom: Whole fried fish with a side of okra and tomato. Courtesy of Reel Fish Coastal Kitchen + Bar.

LEE & RICK'S OYSTER BAR

Old-school seafood house

You could order stuffed flounder at Lee & Rick's. You could also select clam strips, fried fish, "krab" cakes, fried shrimp, or a combo of all four on a platter with fries and slaw. You could, but that would be missing the point. There's one reason that people have come to this industrial corner of Orlovista since 1950, and that's to eat oysters.

The nearest beach is more than sixty miles east, but the minute you board the USS *Lee & Rick's*—this is no metaphor; the restaurant does in fact look like a ship—you'll have no doubt that seafood is what's on tap. Grab a seat at the eighty-foot concrete bar, order a pitcher of beer and a bucket of raw oysters, and then relax and enjoy the show while your shucker gets down to business. Plastic cups of drawn butter, lemon wedges, hot sauce, and sleeve after sleeve of saltines are the only accoutrements here. Once you've slurped your ice-cold oyster from its shell, just toss it into the trough between you and your shucker.

The restaurant had just nine stools and was BYOB when it opened, but otherwise the order of operation remains much the same. Rick Richter was a sailor who had shucked oysters in the Florida Panhandle as a child, and in the early years he drove his pickup to Apalachicola to get the oysters that he and his wife, Lee, served. These days fresh oysters also come from Texas and Louisiana, and they arrive four times a week during the peak oyster months from September to May.

> During high season, Lee & Rick's serves up to two hundred bushels of oysters every week.

Left: Portholes offer a view into the dining room.

Right: Commemorative menus.

Siblings Tricia Richter Blunt and Gene Richter run the place with the same friendly service that their grandparents did. You'll see guests dressed in everything from wet bathing suits to business suits, and that's just fine with the management. While oysters are at the top of the marquee here, the kitchen does a fine job with everything on the menu, from Alaskan snow crab to corn dogs. Steamed peel-and-eat shrimp come with a light dusting of Old Bay Seasoning and offer another tasty way to get messy, but a shrimp shell lacks the proper heft for a good lob over the bar.

5621 Old Winter Garden Rd.
407-293-3587
leeandricksoysterbar.com

Cheesesteaks

There are two big choices to make at Kappy's: whether to dine inside or outside and whether to get the classic cheesesteak or go for Kappy's own version. Both are griddled to order, and if you sit at one of the few swivel stools at the tiny counter, you'll be just a few feet away from said griddle. Each mound of meat and cheese comes on a soft, white sub roll along with whichever combo of grilled onions, mushrooms, and peppers you pick. The classic version features sliced ribeye and provolone; the house twist on the classic combines ground chuck with American cheese.

Locals have been parking right outside the door of this Maitland mainstay since 1967, not only for cheesesteaks but also for cold subs, burgers, dogs, and handmade milk shakes. The vibe here isn't what you'd call retro; it's simply the way it's always been and, hopefully, always will be.

501 N. Orlando Ave., Maitland
407-647-9099
facebook.com/kappyssubs

Cheesesteak at the counter.

Handcrafted Italian cuisine

In the introduction to his cookbook, *9 Courses*, which features his favorite recipes from his Park Avenue restaurants Luma on Park and Prato, Brandon McGlamery sets the table for what to expect as both a reader and a diner: "If you were to walk into Luma on Park or Prato, sit at one of our chef's tables and say, 'Feed me,' the food that followed would likely play out in nine thoughtful courses. It would take at least that many dishes for us to tell our story, show you how we cook, and help you understand the way we approach food in our restaurants."

A Winter Park fave since 2005, Luma on Park is the oldest of the three area restaurants where McGlamery is both chef and partner—Luke's Kitchen and Bar opened a few miles north in Maitland in 2017—but Prato, which opened in 2011, embodies his mindful and modern approach in the warmest and most simple setting. Taking a cue from its park-adjacent location, the contemporary dining room is rich with warm wood and lots of greenery. There's patio seating year-round, but the heart of the space is the long bar running through the middle of the dining room and lending a convivial vibe.

You'll appreciate that communal feel once the food arrives, both because much of it is designed for sharing and because a serious case of order envy is likely no matter what you select. And while it may well take nine courses for you to fully understand the approach, it takes only a few bites to appreciate it. The menu changes seasonally—McGlamery was among the area's first handful of chefs to embrace and promote his use of local ingredients—but always includes a selection of beautifully plated crudo among the antipasti. Expect perfect slices of raw yellowtail with cucumber melon, red grapes, and radish or even a "carne cruda" of beef with a fried egg, charred radicchio, and hazelnut oil.

Above: Prato interior. By Michael Pisarri.

Right: Chef/Partner Brandon McGlamery at his Maitland restaurant, Luke's. By Michael Pisarri.

House-made pastas come in full or half portions, and you'll want to trade bites of butternut squash ravioli with brown butter, currants, ricotta salata, and sage for your companion's egg bucatini with short-rib ragu. Sausages are also made in-house and appear on a Widowmaker pizza along with hazelnut romesco, cavolo nero kale, and a local egg. Share a whole snapper or a thick Berkshire pork chop as a second course and you just might make your way through nine courses after all. If not, there's always next time.

124 N. Park Ave., Winter Park
407-262-0050
prato-wp.com

Orlando landmark for roast beef sandwiches

Ontario native Freeman "Smitty" Smith was forty-three years old when he moved his family to Orlando, but he made up for lost time by quickly creating what would become an Orlando institution. In 1968 he and his wife, Margaret, who was his high school sweetheart, opened the doors to Beefy King. Their son, Roland, and his wife, Sandee, operated it for more than thirty years, and their daughter, Shannon Woodrow, now runs it along with her husband, James.

Just like in '68, sandwiches are made with meats sliced in-house, and staffers pass each portion over the steam vent before piling it on a fresh Kaiser roll with combos of lettuce, onions, slaw, tomato, and cheese. In the tidy Formica dining room, customers help themselves to squeeze bottles of condiments, including barbecue or horseradish sauce, perfect for dousing the moist meat or crunchy tater tots. Turkey, corned beef, barbecue pork, and other meats are also available, but as the sign says, roast beef is king.

424 N. Bumby Ave.
407-894-2241
beefyking.com

Above: Roast beef sandwich and tots. Photo by AaronVan.

Right: The Beefy King sign is an Orlando icon.

THE CATFISH PLACE

Southern seafood

There's a special discount menu for seniors at this mecca for Southern food in St. Cloud, and the lucky diners who can take advantage of it may well have been in their teens when they ate their first fingerlings here. Judy and Steve Johnson opened the doors in 1973, and Judy still runs the place with their children Deana and Randy. To say that it's the area hot spot is an understatement; expect to wait for a table unless you like eating lunch at 11:00 a.m.

Bone-in catfish (fingerlings) are the insider's pick here, but boneless fillets also offer up plenty of sweet flavor from underneath their light cornmeal coating. The folks at the fryer also do a fine job with okra, eggplant, lobster, snapper, and shrimp, as well as pork chops and chicken livers. Diners who crave a full-on Florida experience similar to the one Emeril Lagasse enjoyed when he visited can order a Florida Cracker Special. It comes with fried catfish, frog legs, gator tail, and soft-shell turtle.

2324 Thirteenth St., St. Cloud
407-892-5771
thecatfishplacestcloud.com

The catfish served here is caught on trotlines in Lake Okeechobee. The kitchen fries up more than six thousand pounds of it every week.

Butter beans, a seasonal Southern side, served with fingerlings and hushpuppies.

BLUEBERRIES

Florida foraging

Wild blueberries have grown in Florida since the late 1880s, but commercial production didn't take off until nearly a century later, after scientists from the University of Florida developed cultivars that like long, hot summers. Nowadays there are hundreds of small blueberry farms across the center of the state, and a handful in or near Orange County let you pick your own.

The ideal blueberry is firm and plump and has a shimmery silver bloom on the skin that protects it and keeps it fresh . . . and fresh is what you'll find when you venture forth into the fields with a bucket in hand. Blueberry season begins as early as December, but commercial farms don't typically open for u-pick until the end of the season, typically in April.

A good rule of thumb for u-pick is to call the farm or check its Facebook page before heading out to make sure the weather is on board with your plans. Blueberries and bugs like sun and sandy soil; closed-toe shoes, sunscreen, and bug repellent will save you some heartache. Farms typically rotate the rows that are open for u-pick each day to ensure a steady supply, so all the varieties they grow may not be on offer when you visit. Size, taste, and texture differ depending on the variety, with berries as small as a pea or as large as a quarter and flavors running the gamut from sweet to tart.

> Floridians consume more than 6 percent of the blueberries eaten in the United States.

Bucket of blueberries. Photo by Kristen Manieri.

TRY IT

Beck Brothers is a cash-only u-pick.
12500 Overstreet Rd., Windermere
407-656-4353
facebook.com/beck-brothers-blueberries-u-pick-121170221296165

Chapman's Berries is a cash-only u-pick that also sells
other locally grown products.
75 Nolte Rd., St. Cloud
facebook.com/chapmans-berries-159440454237097

Claire Berries is not far from UCF.
18751 Lake Pickett Rd.
facebook.com/claireberriesblueberryupickfarm

King Grove Organic Farm offers certified organic blueberries.
19714 CR 44A, Eustis
352-589-2469
kinggrove.com

Sand Hill Blueberries is a family-owned farm in Lake County.
31614 Bottany Woods Dr., Eustis
352-636-8204
facebook.com/sandhillblueberries

Southern Hill Farms grows ten varieties of blueberries on
forty acres and has a market and bakery on-site.
Food and beer are available during u-pick weekends.
16651 Schofield Rd., Clermont
407-986-5806
southernhillfarms.com

Tom West Blueberries is run by father-son team Milton and
Scott West. Their berries are a favorite among local chefs.
324 E. Orlando Ave., Ocoee
407-656-3223
tomwestblueberries.com

Top: Sand Hill Blueberries. Photo by Kristen Manieri.

Bottom: Looking for blueberries.

Downtown all-day brasserie

In most parts of the United States, the only eateries that serve breakfast, lunch, and dinner are diners, and at most of them you'd be hard pressed to find a decent glass of wine—not to mention a great one—for toasting a special occasion. But French brasseries are renowned for flowing seamlessly from coffee and croissants in the morning to leisurely business lunches to romantic champagne dinners, and it is this tradition that DoveCote draws from so successfully.

Located downtown on the ground floor of the towering Bank of America Center, DoveCote hums all day long. Foxtail Coffee Co. opens in plenty of time to serve espresso and pastries to the rush-hour crowd, and the natural light streaming in through the enormous Palladian windows energizes many a power luncher enjoying a croque monsieur or an omelet with *fines herbes* and Boursin cheese.

Both the cocktail bar and the raw bar sparkle in the early evening. A shrimp cocktail or a plate of oysters with a barrel-aged cocktail or one of the two dozen or so wines by the glass might be all the dinner you need. It would be a shame, though, to miss chef Clay Miller's wonderful execution of the main menu.

Before coming to Central Florida to become the chef de cuisine at Norman's Orlando, the Pittsburgh native spent years working for such renowned chefs as Daniel Boulud and Thomas Keller. His mastery of technique, dedication to exquisite ingredients, and

The DC Burger has serious panache. It's served with a mayo-based Louie sauce, Boursin cheese, and frisée.

Left: Raw bar and champagne. Photo courtesy of DoveCote.
Right: DoveCote interior windows. Photo courtesy of DoveCote.

approachable style are on full display in classic brasserie dishes, such as hanger steak with frites or a caramelized onion soup. Here the gorgeous gratiné is beefed up with brisket and a touch of fresh horseradish. Miller's personal interpretation of globally influenced French cuisine is also evident in the use of smoked rather than simply roasted eggplant in the escalivada, a traditional dish from the Catalonia region of Spain that borders the south of France.

Weekend brunch is a far more American meal, and accordingly so is the menu. Some of the salads, starters, and sandwiches from the regular menu are offered, along with chocolate-chip pancakes, a crab and Gruyère quiche, and country biscuits with apple jam. Maybe the French could learn a tip or two from us after all.

390 N. Orange Ave.
407-930-1700
dovecoteorlando.com

NEIGHBORHOOD MARKETS

Local produce, proteins, and more

In a region where it can often seem there's a mega-grocery on every corner, it's a treat to stumble into a mom-and-pop kind of place that just seems to magically carry exactly what you want for that evening's dinner. A handful of these independently owned gems are tucked away in tiny plazas all over town and offer a steady supply of locally grown groceries.

The hours they keep may not be quite as accommodating as the chain supermarket, but they're open a lot longer than the typical farmers' market, and while it's unlikely that anyone will offer to walk your enormous cart full of paper towels, cat litter, and other essentials back across the parking lot, you'll meet someone excited to tell you all about the new locally baked goods the shop just started carrying or how to use that organic kohlrabi that a local farmer dropped off. You might even have time to pause and enjoy a kombucha on tap and peruse the latest copy of *Edible Orlando*, a local magazine dedicated to the area's food scene.

TRY IT

A&M Provisions carries local meat from Lake Meadow Naturals, Three Suns Ranch, and Tracy Lee Farms; local pickles, juice, and kombucha; fresh pasta from Trevi Pasta in College Park; dried heirloom beans from Napa-based Rancho Gordo; and an array of gourmet imports from Italy, France, Japan, Greece, and Spain.
2816 Corrine Dr.
407-897-1355
amprovisions.com

Left: Wild Hare is in the heart of downtown Longwood.

Center: Farmacy owners Cathy and Robby Clay. Photo by the Farmacy.

Right: Fresh garlic and Southern olive oils. Photo courtesy of A&M Provisions.

The Farmacy sells fresh produce, eggs, raw milk, and grass-fed meats produced by local and organic farmers chosen by owners Robby and Cathy Clay. As much as 80 percent to 90 percent of their products are locally sourced during peak season.
18 E. Joiner St., Winter Garden
407-921-3912
jointhefarmacy.com

Wild Hare Kitchen & Garden Emporium is a farmers' market and specialty grocery within walking distance of the SunRail station.
335 N. Ronald Reagan Blvd., Longwood
321-203-4535
wildharekitchen.com

Hoover's Market offers more than fourteen thousand grocery items and supplements focusing on organic ingredients.
The family-run market also has a juice bar and café on-site.
1035 Academy Dr., Altamonte Springs
407-869-0000
hooversmarket.com

1940s bungalow bistro

A sign on the small stage of this retro-fabulous Colonialtown bungalow says "Love is all you need." If you prefer love in martini or meatloaf form, then owners Maxine and Kirt Earhart can take care of you too. Beloved for comfort food and cocktails, this warmhearted place is also a showcase for local artists and musicians.

Soothing, grooving, and lighthearted are all words that are used to describe the musical sounds of the soloists and acoustic duos who perform here every weekend. There's also the occasional vaudeville act in the same "sexy and delicious" mode that the Earharts use to describe their vibe. The tagline you'll see on the website and the walls is actually "Sexy Comfortable Delicious," and comfort rules on the menu, especially during Rejucination Brunch. A Warnin' in Da Mornin' cocktail—a Bloody Mary with a beer floater, bacon swizzle, and smoked shrimp and olive skewer—sets the stage for chicken and waffles, crab cakes, or a beef hash made with stout-braised brisket.

337 N. Shine Ave.
407-674-6841
maxinesonshine.com

Top left: Outside Maxine's on Shine.

Top right: Skillet lasagna at Maxine's on Shine.

Bottom: Kirt and Maxine Earhart with a Warnin' in Da Mornin'. Photo courtesy of Maxine's on Shine.

THE BLACK HAMMOCK

Gators, grub, and airboats

People say that gator tastes just like chicken, and they may be right. After all, it can be tough to discern the differences between one fried chunk of white meat and another, but surely everyone can agree that while a gator may taste like a chicken, absolutely no one—not even after several shooters at the Lazy Gator Bar—thinks that a gator *looks* like a chicken.

If you're fuzzy on the particulars of the *Alligator mississippiensis*, just take a gander at the specimens lolling about their enclosure on the Black Hammock's spacious and scenic grounds. There's no fee to look, and you can wander over either before or after your meal, your beer, or your airboat ride. You'd be wise to enjoy your meal after your boat ride, not just because the boat goes awfully fast but also because if you don't see a real live gator during your loop around Lake Jesup, you can console yourself with a sampler of locally raised gator served blackened, Cajun, Buffalo, or Florida style.

2316 Black Hammock Fish Camp Rd., Oviedo
407-365-1244
theblackhammock.com

Owner Joel Martin was born in Paris, grew up in Africa, and immigrated to the United States in 1995.

Top: An airboat ride is delightful before or after eating. Photo courtesy of the Black Hammock.

Bottom: The gator bites gator bites. Photo courtesy of the Black Hammock.

PLANT STREET MARKET

Indoor market, food hall, and brewery

With Crooked Can Brewing Company as the anchor of this hopping retail market with twenty thousand square feet of indoor and outdoor space, you might expect a party vibe all week long. While things here are indeed lively on the weekends, the feel is less beer bash than it is open house. Little Leaguers and their families wander over from the nearby ball fields for a postgame celebration. Children play lawn games on the spacious side patio, while their parents sip a Freedom Ride Stout and look on from a nearby table. Shoppers wander up and down the hall trying to decide between barbecue from This Little Piggy, coal-fired pizza from Michael's Ali, or one of the specialty mac-and-cheeses from Mac'd Out. All food items can be enjoyed anywhere on the premises, making it the perfect spot for a progressive dine.

There are also scores of things to take home, such as the handcrafted artisan chocolates from David Ramirez Chocolates. David Ramirez has been executive pastry chef at Rosen Shingle Creek since 2006, and all his painstakingly meticulous chocolate creations, from red velvet to peanut butter bacon, are made with organic, fair-trade chocolate imported from Europe. There's also a selection of macarons in such flavors as lavender and spiced pistachio.

426 W. Plant St., Winter Garden
786-671-1748
crookedcan.com/plant-st-market

Top: The courtyard at Plant Street Market. Photo courtesy of the City of Winter Garden.

Bottom: A busy day at Plant Street Market. Photo courtesy of the City of Winter Garden.

Thai-style toasted sandwiches

Tea and toasted sandwiches may seem like the menu theme you'd find in an English tea room rather than a spare, cinderblock building near Rollins College, but at this earnest and adorable establishment whose name is the Thai word for Bangkok, that's just what you'll find, but with a Thai twist.

Basil, onion, cilantro, and—for an additional twenty-five cents—Thai chilies all lend zest to various signature sandwiches. Fillings are nestled between slices of artisan bread from Olde Hearth Bread Company and married with a melty slice of fromage; the Larb combines marinated chicken, red onion, mint leaves, cilantro, and spicy roasted-lime sauce with mozzarella. All sandwiches are served with a salad, and some also come *as* a salad, a.k.a. a naked sandwich.

More than thirty tea varieties are on the list, which includes tasting notes, origin, and level of caffeine. Most of the teas pair just as well with savories as they do with sweets, and desserts are also toast-centric. Thick slices of "brick toast" are topped with goodies such as organic honey, matcha and green-tea ice cream (Cha-Cha), crushed peanut, condensed milk, and coconut ice cream (Ka-Ti), and more. High Hats are upside-down sundaes—lighter on carbs but not on comfort.

1051 W. Fairbanks Ave., Winter Park
407-733-3561
krungthepteatime.com

Strawberry cheesecake at Krungthep Tea Time. Photo by Marta Madigan.

Café, grocery, and bakery

One of the more popular punches in the Caribbean is named for its main ingredient, sorrel, which is the Jamaican word for hibiscus. The dried flowers are used to make a ruby-red tea flavored with fresh ginger, orange zest, cinnamon, and typically an awful lot of sugar. (Think of it as Jamaican sweet tea.) This same spiky variety of hibiscus also flourishes in Florida—some savvy marketers have even begun to refer to it as Florida cranberry—and you can sometimes find fresh buds at local farmers' markets. At Caribbean Sunshine, you can buy dried sorrel by the bag in addition to the spicy house-made potable version.

While you're there, you'll notice lots of other ingredients that are familiar to any Floridian, such as okra, snapper, and shrimp. You'd be hard-pressed to find fresh callaloo outside of a Caribbean grocery store, but darned if the leafy greens don't taste like a more delicate collard. Here it makes a fine breakfast sautéed with onion and saltfish, toothsome flakes of the same salt cod known as bacalao in Puerto Rico. Another popular breakfast served here is saltfish with ackee, Jamaica's national fruit. Ackee does not grow in Florida, but much of the fun in coming here is the chance to try new things.

Of course, the patties, jerk chicken, and curry goat aren't new at all to the scores of regulars who come here for a taste of home. All three locations are low-frills, and in each you order at the palm-thatched counter. The newest location in Winter Garden—it opened

> Many of the punches and cakes that originated as Christmas treats in the islands are now enjoyed year-round.

Left: Customers order at the counter at Caribbean Sunshine. Photo by AaronVan.

Right: A breakfast of callaloo with saltfish, plantains, sweet potatoes, and boiled dumplings. Photo by AaronVan.

in 2008; the first opened in 1992—is the only spot with outdoor seating. The West Colonial location is inside a hidden mini-mall, where you can enjoy your packed-to-bursting Styrofoam clamshell within eyeshot of the adjacent vendors' wares; the most colorful are the bikinis adorned with various Caribbean national flags.

The bakery puts out classic versions of island breads, such as Jamaican coco bread, Guyanese tennis rolls, and molasses-laden loaves of Jamaican bulla cake. There are also slabs of coconut cake and slices of rich, black rum cake and red velvet cake as deeply hued as that sorrel drink. For both first-time and longtime visitors, this taste of the islands is a sweet escape from the rest of the city.

2528 W. Colonial Dr.
407-839-5060

6922 Silver Star Rd.
407-578-0068

16112 Marsh Rd., Winter Garden
407-654-6625

caribbeansunshinebakery.net

HOLLERBACH'S WILLOW TREE CAFÉ

German restaurant plus a market and outfitters

Theo Hollerbach may not be the elected mayor of Sanford, but he's certainly the most visible denizen of downtown's Historic District, even when he's not strolling the square in lederhosen. When he and his wife, Linda, opened the Willow Tree Café on downtown's main drag in 2001, they had just seven employees, and there was little to lure visitors to the scrappy area that was once celebrated as Celery City. Once customers started coming to sample the schnitzel, though, they kept coming back, and the Hollerbachs expanded their businesses while other new eateries and retailers sprouted up around them. These days the Hollerbachs run their growing empire with the help of their daughter Christina and a whopping ninety employees.

The Willow Tree Café isn't the only reason to visit downtown Sanford, but it's still the biggest draw. At lunchtime the covered patio and the open dining room festooned with European flags are filled with both area businesspeople and folks killing time before catching the nearby Auto Train to head north. Tables fill up with families and revelers hungry for German-style wursts, boots of German beer, and, Thursdays through Sundays, the foot-stomping sounds of Jimmy and Eckhard. This musical duo brings serious *gemütlichkeit*—the German word for happiness, friendliness, and coziness all bundled in one—along with an accordion, alpine bells, spoons, and a singing saw.

Ladies need not wear a dirndl to dine in this festive place, but those who desire one can simply walk around the corner to

Left: Live music and dancing in Magnolia Square during Oktoberfest. Photo courtesy of Hollerbach's Willow Tree Café.

Right: Eisbein with sauerkraut and heaven-and-earth potatoes. Photo courtesy of Hollerbach's Willow Tree Café.

Hollerbach's Outfitters for a full selection of traditional German folkwear for damen, herren, and kinder. You'll see these fashions out in full force during Hollerbach's weekend-long outdoor Oktoberfest celebration, which brings more than fifteen thousand partiers to the streets of Sanford each year.

Many of the ingredients and menu items for sale in the café are also available at Magnolia Square Market. The long deli case has pride of place in this well-stocked German grocery, and deli meats and imported cheeses are sold by the pound or on a sandwich made with freshly baked bread. Little ones will thrill over the store's selection of Haribo gummis, marzipan, and German chocolates; the twenty-one-plus crowd can partake in a vast selection of German and Austrian beers and wines. You can enjoy all the market's specialties inside or outdoors with a view of Magnolia Square and its fountain. *Gemütlichkeit*, indeed.

205 E. First St., Sanford
407-321-2204
hollerbachs.com

UK rock-and-roll motor diner

The Orlando outpost of the UK-based Ace Café has been a long time coming. The original location on London's North Circular Road was opened in 1938 as a low-key eatery for travelers and truckers. Its location soon attracted motorcyclists as well, and those bikers and "ton-up boys" embodied the rowdy rock-and-roll vibe that defined the place up until it closed in 1969. On the twenty-fifth anniversary of its closure, Mark Wilsmore arranged a music-and-motorcycle event at the old site that drew more than twelve thousand enthusiasts; in 2001 the Ace Café was back in business and as boisterous as ever.

Ace Café has grown to include a handful of locations in Europe and one in Beijing, but our downtown is home to what is currently the only place in the United States to indulge a craving for speed thrills and a global menu of backroads grub. Fuel up with hearty chicken soup and chili, wings, burgers, and comforting entrées, such as Bat Outta Hell Meatloaf wrapped in bacon and served with tomato-bacon jam, onion gravy, and garlic mashed potatoes. And, of course, there's a shout-out to the Ace's British heritage: George's Fish & Chips are made with North Atlantic haddock fried in house-made Yuengling beer batter and served with steak fries and mushy peas.

100 W. Livingston St.
407-996-6686
acecafeusa.com

Nearly every night sees Ace's parking lot packed with meets of motorcycles, muscle cars, or Euro cars; music on the weekends is live and loud.

166

Top: Motorcycle meet. Photo courtesy of Ace Café.

Bottom: George's fish and chips. Photo courtesy of Ace Café.

Peruvian seafood and more

There are as many ways to spell ceviche—or seviche or cebiche—as there are to make it, but the Peruvians are credited with creating that first dish of raw seafood "cooked" in citrus juice. Variations abound throughout Latin America, but the simplest versions include just one type of seafood chopped up with little more than onions and cilantro.

The ceviche de pescado here is just that, with garlic and red rocoto pepper added to the base. Ceviche de camarones and ceviche de pulpo give the same treatment to shrimp and octopus, respectively, but offerings beyond these basics are a lively mix of flavors and textures. A cold appetizer of chores a la Chalaca, or mussels served in the style of the Peruvian port of Callao, comes with huge white kernels of Peruvian corn and an optional topping of chopped octopus.

While the name of this homey restaurant not far from Gatorland may suggest that the menu is dominated by raw seafood, ceviche is just one of the many authentic Peruvian dishes that are available here. Seafood also comes fried, poached in fish broth, or sautéed with onions, tomatoes, and white wine. Peruvians also love meat, and lomo saltado is a national favorite featuring stir-fried strips of beef tenderloin with onions and tomatoes. Here you can also enjoy it a lo pobre, with a fried egg and sweet plantains, or in a tacu tacu with crispy fried rice and beans.

The ancient Incas were the first to cultivate potatoes thousands of years ago, and many people believe that the causa, a mashed potato terrine layered with meat or seafood, is at least as old. For first-time

More than four thousand varieties of potato are native to Peru and mostly found in the Andes.

Top left: An appetizer of Peruvian-style mussels. Photo by Michael Lothrop.

Bottom left: Fish ceviche with Peruvian corn, or *choclo*. Photo by Michael Lothrop.

Right: Causa made with chicken salad at Ceviche House. Photo by Michael Lothrop.

diners, the dish will seem at once foreign and familiar; cold mashed potatoes are not typically a thing in North American cuisine, but one bite will have you thinking that perhaps they should be. Here, layers of smooth, whipped Yukon gold and red potatoes sandwich a layer of either chicken, tuna, or mixed seafood salad bound with garlic aioli and topped with a sauce made from black Peruvian botija olives.

For dessert there are Peruvian sandwich cookies called alfajores, made with cornstarch and filled with dulce de leche. Ice creams are flavored with cherimoya, soursop, or lucuma.

12213 S. Orange Blossom Tr.
407-812-1717
cevicheorlando.com

Small-batch bakery and café

Absolutely no one was surprised when this bijou bakery was an immediate success when it opened in 2014. After all, for the previous two years, Lana Rebroff and her children, daughter Taissa and son Philip, had built a cult following at the Audubon Park Community Market. They regularly sold out of their sweet and savory double-baked croissants, key lime pie Pop-Tarts, and buttery tea cakes long before the evening's end. What may have been a surprise to some, though, is that this tight-knit team is as skilled at preparing hearty lunch and brunch fare as it is at the delicate art of Viennoiserie.

Even dishes that are de rigueur on café menus have a special twist or two here. A thick slice of house-made country sourdough is the base for lemony avocado toast sprinkled with sprouts and a healthy dash of dukkah, an Egyptian blend of ground herbs, nuts, and spices. The gravy atop the buttermilk biscuits is made with roasted mushrooms and black pepper, and rye pancakes are topped with warm apple compote and sour cream.

Opening a bakery together wasn't always part of the Rebroff family's plan. A year or so after graduating from UCF, Taissa moved to New York to work as a freelance writer. She ended up with a job at a Brooklyn bakery and learned that she loved baking as much as

> "We have so many regular customers, and we've seen so many kids grow up throughout the years, that it feels like we're truly a part of people's lives. Our building is from 1925, and I think that its quirks make it a cozy space (if a little creaky)."
> – Taissa Rebroff

Left: Patio at Buttermilk Bakery. Photo by Jamie Thompson.

Right: Buttermilk Bakery. Photo by Jamie Thompson.

her mom and brother did. Back in Central Florida, the trio found the farmers' market to be the perfect platform for getting their goods out there, and wholesale sales to small businesses, such as Farm & Haus and Lineage Coffee Roasting, provided the needed support to solidify their plans for a brick-and-mortar shop.

After you order at the counter, it's lovely to sit inside the spare, sunlit room and watch other customers try to decide between the traditional kouign-amann—a sugary parcel of layered croissant dough with a crunchy crust—or the dark-chocolate version. On nice days, though, the small deck on the side is the place to be. One area resident was so taken with the spot that he staged a proposal there. His delighted fiancée shared the news with her Instagram followers through a post of her newly jeweled hand intertwined with his but still close to her chocolate croissant.

1198 Orange Ave., Winter Park

321-422-4015

buttermilk-bakery.com

INTERNATIONAL FOOD CLUB

Global grocery store

When the proprietors of this online store and warehouse retail space chose to describe their stock as international, they weren't kidding—pastas, oils, pulses, spices, sweets, snacks, coffee, wine, and beer are imported from more than fifty countries all over the world. There are many excellent international markets in Orlando, but most specialize in products from a specific region. Here you'll find what is easily the widest variety of imported goods in town.

A trip to the freezer section alone is a lesson in both gastronomy and geography. British bangers share shelf space with pierogies and pelmeni stuffed with meat, potatoes, mushrooms, or sauerkraut, just a few steps down from the samosas. Nonperishables are stacked throughout the center of the store and include olives by the pound as well as jarred pickles made from eggplant, peppers, turnips, and lemon.

The Middle Eastern offerings make up a large share of the vast selection, and while imports from pomegranate molasses to canned fava beans are fun finds, it's the locally made traditional items that are the real treasures here. A new outpost for Winter Springs–based Saba Bakes offers an array of Iranian sweets and savories, and among the long tables piled high with flatbreads from Village Bread & Bagel in Jacksonville are savories from Cedars Bakery right down the street. In addition to traditional pita bread, this mostly wholesale bakery also makes sfeeha, which are Lebanese pies stuffed with combinations of meat, cheese, and spinach.

During lunch you can also enjoy a world of tastes from the on-site café. The regular menu features tabouleh wraps, kebabs, gyros,

Left: Prepared foods are available to go or stay. Photo by Robert Bangiola.
Right: UK specialties in the freezer at International Food Club.

samosas, and more than a dozen sides, including two kinds of beans: British baked beans and giant Greek white beans. Daily specials circle the globe for savories, such as chicken tikka masala or Caribbean-style calypso chicken.

While it's wise to budget an hour for exploring and eating, if you're short on time you can get the trip in a nutshell with a visit to the refrigerated room near the register. Here you'll find the store's entire selection of wine, beer, and chocolates, with lots of great gift items available. Anglophiles will drool over Bassett's bonbons and Fry's chocolates; fans of offbeat wines will be pleased to find bottles from Greece and Russia, as well as imported sherries and vermouth.

4300 LB McLeod Rd.
321-281-4300
internationalfoodclub.com

Puerto Rican sweets and savory specialties

Whether you choose to linger over a café con leche or grab a sandwich to go at Eduardo Colón and Denisse Janira Torres's Kissimmee bakery, you're going to have to wait in line. Possibly two lines, actually. Hot food is ordered through a cafeteria-style line on one side, where staffers dish up ready-to-go dishes and take orders for made-to-order sandwiches and other items. Grab a seat and wait to hear your order shouted out over the open room, or spend your wait time in the other line, where you can buy bread, pastries, cakes, and flans from a separate cashier. This can be confusing for a first-time visitor, but with more than two thousand customers at this location every day, the staff here has the crowd control down to a science.

Something beyond science, however, explains the appeal of this hospitable hub for the Latino community. The Colons named their business after Vega Baja (a.k.a. La Ciudad del Melao Melao), a Puerto Rican city renowned for producing the island's sweetest sugar cane, and that sweetness pervades even their savory dishes. There is love in the mofongo, a traditional dish that includes a dense dome of fried green plantains mashed with pork cracklings, garlic, and olive oil. Here you can choose between versions with chicken, steak, shrimp, pork, or tilapia with either garlic sauce or a criolla (Creole) sauce made with bell peppers, tomato, and onion.

> "Through our cuisine, customers have come to understand our feelings and the joy we bring as Puerto Ricans."
> – Denisse Janira Torres

Left: Shrimp mofongo. Photo by Michael Lothrop.

Right: The hot line at Melao Bakery. Photo by Michael Lothrop.

There are several fried and stuffed snacks popular throughout Latin America, but alcapurrias are specific to Puerto Rico. The long, peg-shaped fritters are made from either shredded green banana or yucca and filled with mildly seasoned ground beef. Sandwiches here are pressed on Puerto Rican pan de agua, sweet medianoche (midnight) bread, or eggy Mallorcan bread. Classic Cuban combos are available along with more American-style tuna salad, pastrami, or bacon and cheese.

The Orlando location is every bit as busy, and those looking for a taste of home are just as likely to be tourists, but both locations offer plenty to try—if you're willing to wait.

1912 Fortune Rd., Kissimmee
2001 Consulate Dr.
407-348-1777
melaobakery.com

JIMOTTI'S RESTAURANT

Suburban izakaya

It's hard to imagine a more unlikely spot for a chef with Junichi Takazoe's experience to hang up a shingle, but this odd A-frame building on a charmless stretch of 17-92 is just where he landed, and Sanford residents couldn't be happier to have him in their backyard. Since 2016, this humble spot that looks like an old drive-in is the place for homestyle cooking from a chef who worked in some of the most renowned sushi restaurants in Japan and LA before coming to Orlando to work with the start-up team at Morimoto Asia at Disney Springs.

While Takazoe is a master of presentation and favors organic ingredients and high-quality meats and seafood, his menu is as decidedly down to earth as the restaurant itself. "Jimotti" is Japanese slang for local people, and the casually dressed groups of locals who trickle in and out are all taken care of by a lone server. Classic rock blares from the kitchen during both lunch and dinner, and you'll often see one or two of Takazoe's four daughters doing homework or amusing themselves at a table near the kitchen.

Chalkboard sushi specials and entrées, such as grilled local fish or organic pork chops, are available along with the regular menu at lunch and dinner, but rice bowls topped with braised beef, salmon, and tuna poke or spicy tuna with Japanese style "kara-ague" fried chicken are only available during lunch. Happy hour is the perfect time for getting to know the menu, with starters of kara-ague chicken, grilled Japanese black-pork sausages, and select rolls on special, along with the conversation starter called Take a Chance. Here hollowed jalepeño peppers are stuffed with spicy tuna and lightly fried. One, however, still contains its fiery seeds.

More than a dozen varieties of traditional ramen and udon soups are also available. Two less common broth-free udon dishes are on

Left: Some diners consider hamachi kama, or yellowtail collar, the tastiest part of the fish.

Top right: The udon aglio e olio is a Japanese twist on an Italian classic.

Bottom right: The juicy Angus burger is only available during dinner.

the menu: the thick white noodles in the mentai caviar udon are sauced with soy sauce and butter and topped with green onion, seaweed, and spicy Pollock roe, while Takazoe's twist on garlicky Italian pasta aglio e olio adds a bit of heat along with tender chunks of shrimp and squid.

Given Takazoe's background, there is, of course, a superb if small selection of sushi here, and all of it hews to the most classic of presentations. As with the building itself, there's no need to put on airs here to impress diners.

2545 S. French Ave., Sanford
407-952-3329
jimotti.com

Venezuelan diner

The people smiling back from the dozens of framed photos along the long wall of this cozy diner in a Publix plaza south of Sea World look almost as happy as the people actually eating there. Turnover is brisk at the bank of booths along the counter, where staffers in black-and-rainbow #orlandounited T-shirts pull espressos; stuff arepas with meat, cheese, or chicken; and bag to-go orders. A few stools along the short side of the counter allow for a bird's-eye view of the friendly and efficient staff and their happy customers.

The kitchen in back grills the steaks, chops, and sausages that come on platters with rice and beans, but the patacón, or plantain sandwich, is the biggest draw. This Venezuelan specialty utilizes slices of fried green or sweet plantains in lieu of bread and fills each sandwich with beef, chicken, or pork along with lettuce, tomato, and cheese.

8117 Vineland Ave.
407-238-0014
facebook.com/elautenticosaborvenezolano

A milk shake-thick chicha is a richly sweet drink made with rice, milk, sugar, and cinnamon.

Top: Behind the busy counter at Q'Kenan.

Bottom: Families enjoying Sunday lunch at Q'Kenan.

Fiery Chinese food

The menu at Spicy Girl is not for the faint of heart, and neither is its location. It is located in a Howard Johnson that has seen much better days—and saw them very long ago—and the best way to find this no-frills spot for fiery food is by looking for the Open House signs that have been Sharpied with Chinese characters and following the arrows to the parking lot around back. Once you make it, your reward is some of the tastiest Sichuan-style food that the area has to offer, spicy and otherwise.

Chaoshou are large dumplings popular in Sichuan, and the name literally translates to "folded hands." Here the folded dumplings come in a soup doused in chili oil. Other soups include pork noodle or a hot-and-sour soup with rice noodles and beef that is much heartier and more complex than the complimentary pre-meal cup that American diners will have sampled in a less authentic restaurant.

Equally authentic and also hard to find are the rice flour dishes. These mildly spiced steamed dishes enclose a center of chopped and ground meat with potatoes in a thick layer of pounded rice similar in texture to polenta, resulting in Chinese comfort food anyone can enjoy.

4311 W. Vine St., Kissimmee
321-732-1749

Top: A Spicy Girl rice powder special with mutton.

Bottom: Spicy noodles at Spicy Girl.

STICKY RICE LAO STREET FOOD

Orlando's only Lao restaurant

Street food in general is meant to be eaten with your fingers, and sticky rice might be the most fun way to dine with your digits. This highly glutinous rice is a staple of Laos, where it's the basis of every meal and the first thing a young cook learns to master. One thing is certain. Chef/owner Kevin Phanhvilay has nailed the technique, along with mastering the other snack-sized offerings here.

At this Mills 50 restaurant that's done up to look like a market stall inside, you order at the counter and take a seat at one of the long communal tables. Plastic bags of sticky rice are meant to be ordered on the side along with dips and meat entrées. A dip trio is a good intro to Lao flavors and includes cups of charred tomato sauce (jeow mak len), sweet chili paste with pork skin (jeow bong), and lime chile sauce (jeow som). Or, use the sticky rice to scoop up bites of larb gai, seasoned ground chicken with herbs, toasted rice, and cucumber. Phanhvilay's favorite accompaniment to sticky rice is his lemongrass beef jerky, and with most of the menu items priced at less than five bucks, you can easily try most of the options before declaring your own personal pick.

Another sticky specialty is sakoo sai moo, spherical tapioca dumplings made with minced pork and sweet radish and garnished with peanuts. Flavorful grilled chicken wings come with their own handle, as do skewers of house-made meatballs with sweet chili sauce or grilled coconut beef in a lemongrass marinade. Feel free to use actual utensils for digging out the good stuff from a bowl of khao poon nam gai: rice vermicelli and chicken in a coconut curry broth.

Top left: Satisfying chicken soup comes with house-made rice noodles. Photo courtesy of Sticky Rice Lao Street Food.

Bottom left: From left, lemongrass pork sausages, sesame beef jerky, and pork tapioca dumplings. Photo courtesy of Sticky Rice Lao Street Food.

Right: Beerlao is the perfect balance for a spicy laab made with steak, chicken, or mushrooms. Photo courtesy of Sticky Rice Lao Street Food.

Just as in Thai cuisine, rich, meaty Lao dishes are tempered by the tartness of a salad. You can order spicy servings of papaya or cucumber salad with regular, hot, or "Lao hot" levels of heat. Should you happen to go overboard on spice, sweet and starchy desserts featuring combos of coconut crème and ripe mango with—you guessed it, sticky rice—should cool the flames.

1915 E. Colonial Dr.
321-800-6532
facebook.com/stickyricestreetfood

CLADDAGH COTTAGE IRISH PUB

Imported beers and house-made food

This isn't the first incarnation of the Irish pub where owners Vicki Gish and Scott Vocca met in 2000 during a traditional Irish music session. They bought the business in early 2016 and just three months later learned that the building was being sold and that they'd have to vacate the handsome building where they'd fallen in love. Talk about pluck, though—in just two years the couple re-created the Claddagh Cottage a mile away, right down to the red door and the wood beams, and they are pulling pints and playing music in the Hourglass District once again.

A fireplace isn't exactly a necessity in Florida's climate, but it—along with the dartboards, white plaster walls, and Guinness mirror behind the bar—sure does make the place feel like home. And home is where you can get a perfect pint and a comforting bowl of potato and leek soup. You can eat a pasty with one hand while you slap your knee with the other during live music on the weekends and traditional Irish sessions every other Wednesday.

2421 Curry Ford Rd.
407-895-1555
claddaghcottagepub.com

The heart, hands, and crown on the Claddagh ring symbolize love, friendship, and loyalty.

Above: Outside Claddagh Cottage.

Left: A perfect pint. Photo by Cathy Agnew.

ARARAT EURO FOOD & BISTRO

Eastern European market and restaurant

It shouldn't be surprising to find an international market and restaurant in the shadow of ICON Orlando 360, the giant Ferris wheel whose imperceptible rotations seem to echo the earth itself. The whole area is as packed with Brazilian superstores, hookah lounges, and Indian buffets as it is tourists. The offerings at this market and bistro, however, seem geared to the community of Eastern Europeans who actually live in Central Florida.

In addition to an impressive cache of caviar, the market sells everyday items, such as breads from Lithuania, Germany, and the Ukraine; an array of wood-smoked fish; spreads, sauces, and pickles from throughout Eastern Europe; and more than fifty traditional varieties of sausages, smoked meat, cheeses, and pate. Customers could easily grab everything needed for a traditional meal here, or better yet walk a few steps over to the bistro half of the building and enjoy the most extensive selection of Eastern European dishes available in Orlando.

On weekends, the few booths that provide the only indoor seating fill up with families who have reserved in advance, but you may be able to score a spot outside or outside of peak times without calling first. This is a meal to plan ahead for because you'll want to bring your appetite and plenty of friends so you can try as many dishes as possible. Such soups as mushroom cream and traditional borscht with beets and cabbage are among the starters that will feel familiar

Solyanka is a meaty sweet-and-sour soup made with pickles and olives and garnished with lemon and sour cream.

Left: Chicken tabaka features a whole seared Cornish game hen.

Center: A board of salo, cured pork fatback, at Ararat.

Right: Cabbage rolls are served with sour cream and housemade sweet-and-sour sauce.

to first-time diners. Both are scratch made and delicious, but you'll find the most interesting options for kicking off your meal among the salads and cold appetizers.

In addition to the raw vegetable salads that Americans will recognize are a number of chilled combinations featuring pickles, cooked vegetables, bologna, and smoked fish. Salo is a sharable cold starter, and the butcher's board comes laden with thin slices of cured pork fatback and garnishes of pickles, garlic, green onion, and grilled bread. Grilled chops and skewered meats, or shashlik, are simple and satisfying; cabbage rolls stuffed with ground beef are baked in a zippy house-made sweet-and-sour sauce. Vegetarians could easily make a meal of hot appetizers, such as kasha with mushrooms, eggplant cutlets with yogurt-walnut sauce, and potato or zucchini pancakes.

While you wait, enjoy an Armenian yogurt drink, a glass of dry white wine from the nation of Georgia, or a Czech beer and watch Russian music videos on the overhead television.

7540 Universal Blvd.

407-351-3131

ararateuro.com

Downtown hotel restaurant

Downtown Orlando wouldn't feel like a proper downtown without a grand hotel, so it's a good thing that the Grand Bohemian is there to make things right. Just across the lawn from the Dr. Phillips Center for the Performing Arts, its artful lobby is every bit as theatrical as the Broadway tours that come to town, and the Imperial Grand Bösendorfer Piano that has pride of place in the rotunda is the icing on top of this very ornate cake. The stunning white piano is no mere showpiece, however; it's put to tuneful use during Sunday Jazz Brunch, when diners indulge in mimosas and Boheme Benedicts.

Even without live music, the rich red main dining room just off the rotunda engages all the senses. It's tempting to trail your fingers across a wall of floor-to-ceiling fringe on the way to your table. Once seated, you can rest your palms on the cool marble tabletop and sink into your red leather armchair. Dinner is a Continental affair—as in the continent of Europe—and even when the dining room is at peak capacity, the pace of each meal is unrushed.

Executive Chef Laurent Hollaender is from Strasbourg, the largest city in the historic region of Alsace that sits on the French side of the German border. His European tastes and technique are on display in such starters as the escargots de Bourgogne or a "hunter's board" of Italian speck and soppressata, truffle chicken liver mousse, cheeses, and lingonberry jam. Aged steaks get a peppery rub that pairs wonderfully with a smooth side of truffle potato puree; an entrée of sea bass is a guest favorite, featuring a thick white fillet of fish with a puree of butternut squash, cucumber radish salad, and a lemon beurre blanc with riesling.

If you're not dashing off to make an 8:00 p.m. curtain, consider a digestif in the Bösendorfer Lounge. Once the pre-theater crowds

Above: The dining room at the Boheme. Photo courtesy of Grand Bohemian Orlando.

Right: A sea bass entrée. Photo courtesy of Grand Bohemian Orlando.

clear, you might get a seat at the circular bar, where you can watch the mixologists at work. Or choose a window seat and people-watch along Orange Avenue. After all, you are downtown.

Grand Bohemian Hotel Orlando
325 S. Orange Ave.
407-581-4700
kesslercollection.com/boheme-restaurant

Food made with passion and Florida ingredients

There are so many hybrid forms of chic—shabby chic, urban chic, farmhouse chic—that we can sometimes forget that the best version is unadulterated and effortless. The dining room at Julie and James Petrakis's flagship Winter Park restaurant is just that: chic. The backs of tufted tan leather banquettes come halfway up a wall that looks as if a group of abstract artists have stood on the seats to paint directly on the wall. On the other side of the room, large pieces of monochromatic green, red, and gold artwork hang from a pipe affixed to the half wall that separates the dining room from the bar. Down the middle, sleek lighted columns soar between tables in the back-to-back rows, making each party feel as if the space in the room is theirs alone.

That same simplicity rules the menu, where bold-face main ingredients star in careful combinations that feel approachable without stooping to pander. When the owners opened the Pig in 2007, the two Culinary Institute of America grads were not entirely sure that their hometown would embrace their ethos of sustainable food made with local ingredients. Their gamble paid off, however, and the restaurant is a local darling that has been nominated for a James Beard Award and received accolades from many national media outlets.

The menu changes seasonally according to the availability of ingredients, but diners can always expect a pub burger and truffle fries, a farmer salad with Florida produce, or a Friday-only offering of Birds and Bubbles, a prix-fixe menu that pairs fried chicken for two with a bottle of sparkling wine. Fall might bring a medley of roasted and pureed vegetables from Tomazin Farms or Frog

Left: Bartender with clarified milk punch at the Ravenous Pig.

Top right: Shrimp and grits. Photo courtesy of the Ravenous Pig.

Bottom right: Pigtails. Photo courtesy of the Ravenous Pig.

Song Organics along with a firm white fillet of tripletail from Port Canaveral, or venison carpaccio with compressed heirloom apples, hibiscus, chestnut aioli, and orange-chestnut gremolata.

House-made charcuterie is a mainstay at lunch, dinner, and weekend brunch, where rock shrimp tacos seem every bit as Southern as the Southern Benedict, which combines braised pork with candied collards and a red-eye hollandaise. After a meal here, you won't care whether the fare is gastropub or farm-to-table. You'll just call it good.

565 W. Fairbanks Ave., Winter Park
407-628-2333
theravenouspig.com

Rooftop steakhouse, bar, and tapas

Orlando offers myriad opportunities to indulge in dinner theater, both literal (interactive murder mysteries, jousting matches) and figurative (towering milk shakes adorned with cake, skewers of meat carved tableside). There are fewer places to enjoy what one might call dinner drama. Enter Capa, located on the seventeenth floor of the dramatic-in-its-own-right Four Seasons Resort.

At this steakhouse inspired by the Basque region of Spain, diners in the striking and spare black dining room can choose to visit the kitchen for a peek at chefs working the wood-fired grill, look up at the ceiling to see the swirling red sculpture by Dutch artist Peter Gentenaar, or gaze across the terrace where Disney fireworks explode into view each evening. A glittering mural of antique coins lends sparkle to the bar, which also opens onto the terrace.

The menu also lends itself to simple yet bold statements. Aperitifs pair well with a dozen or so tapas, such as bacon-wrapped dates with almonds, maple, and tamarind or ham croquettes with salbitxada, a sauce from Catalonia made with charred green onions. There's also a selection of Spanish cheeses and charcuterie, including the world-renowned jamón de Bellota, obtained from acorn-fed black-footed Iberico pigs.

There's an Iberico pork chop on the grill menu, along with a la carte offerings of lamb, lobster, and prime steaks, including Wagyu beef from Japan. The accompanying mound of finishing salt and a charred pepper or two are all that's needed to perfect the thirty-two-ounce porterhouse for two, but you can take it higher with one of a handful of house-made Spanish-style sauces on the menu.

Top left: Capa porterhouse for two. Photo by Don Riddle.

Top right: Overhead view the signature Capa Gin Tonic. Photo by Don Riddle.

Bottom: The dining room at Capa. Photo by Don Riddle.

Desserts pay homage to the Spanish love for chocolate. Valor chocolates have been produced in Spain since 1881, and here they appear in the form of a chocolate mousse with coffee ice cream and toffee crunch. If you time your reservation accordingly, you can get a side of Mouse with your mousse; your server will let you know when the fireworks are about to begin and invite you to step out onto the terrace to enjoy the show. Dinner theater at its finest.

Four Seasons Resort Orlando at Walt Disney World Resort
10100 Dream Tree Blvd.
407-313-7777
fourseasons.com/orlando/dining/restaurants/capa

Fine Mexican fare, mezcal, and tequila

The first thought most people have when they walk into a restaurant is not typically, "Hmm, I could live here." If that restaurant is Reyes Mezcaleria, however, you might begin contemplating having your mail forwarded or at the very least booking a private event. Sue Chin's contemporary coastal design for the restaurant that she owns with her husband, Jason, is so very inviting—especially the lounge, which is kitted out with vintage rattan, ferns, and macramé—that you'll feel as if you've wandered into your own personal Pinterest board.

The beautiful bar beckons, however, and your reward for prying yourself out of that crushed-velvet armchair is a lengthy list of fine tequilas and mezcal, another agave-based spirit from Mexico that has a distinct flavor because of its production process. If you're new to the taste, try it blended in a Oaxacan Old Fashioned along with tequila and house-made mole bitters. Bar bites include pork rinds with lime aioli and sometimes chipotle-roasted grasshoppers.

In the kitchen, Executive Chef Wendy Lopez and her team create regional Mexican specialties, such as the hamachi tostada, which tops slices of the cured fish with salmon roe, lime aioli, and crushed peanut chile oil. Squash is spiced up in a roasted and grilled assortment served with house-made mole and warm tortillas, and a tamale of wild mushrooms and poblano peppers is served with tomatillo salsa and crema. Line-caught snapper is available whole or as a fillet, with a Veracruz-style sauce of roasted tomatoes, olives, capers, and lemon.

Mexican cuisine is only the newest undertaking for the Chins, who also own two successful restaurants across the street from one another in Baldwin Park: Seito Sushi and Osprey Tavern, which features new American cuisine. Maybe it's the mezcal talking, but despite its more urban location, this spot has the most homelike feel.

Top: Tostada with cured hamachi, salmon roe, lime aioli, and crushed peanut chili oil. Photo courtesy of Reyes Mezcaleria.

Bottom left: Chipotle-roasted grasshoppers and mezcal. Photo courtesy of Reyes Mezcaleria.

Bottom right: Inside the lounge. Photo courtesy of Reyes Mezcaleria.

821 N. Orange Ave.
407-868-9007
reyesmex.com

Nine seats, many courses

The term "forever home" is the phrase that college friends Lordfer Lalicon, Jennifer Bañagale, and Mark V. Berdin use to describe the boxy black building that is their sushi and sake bar. The trio of University of Florida alums started out with a sushi stand, Kappo, inside East End Market a few doors down but closed it to focus on their ambitious and extremely popular endeavor. With just nine seats in the entire place, Orlandoans can only hope it stays forever so that everyone can partake.

To experience Kadence, you must go online to book a seat for an eighteen-course sushi and sashimi tasting menu, a smaller early-bird tasting, or a lunch consisting of twelve pieces of sushi served piece by piece along with soup and dessert. Reservations are prepaid only and include tax and tip along with the menu, which is chosen by the chefs and focuses on the highest-quality selection of seasonal fish. All three chefs at Kadence are Certified Advanced Sake Professionals and each evening offer a tasting of three, five, or seven different sakes that pair with the meal. You can purchase a sake tasting when booking online, or you can decide when you arrive and pay at the end of the meal.

1809 E. Winter Park Rd.
kadenceorlando.com

Above: Mark V. Berdin puts the finishing touches on a chilled oyster.

Boutique artisan bakery

Stacey and Ed Tomljenovich have both loved to cook and bake for as long as they can remember, but until the fall of 2015, when they bought a beloved local bakery from its original owner, neither of them had done so professionally. So they kept the original recipes for the pies, pie pops, cutie pies, and hand pies that the small batch artisan bakery was known for while continuing to make everything from scratch and use seasonal and local ingredients whenever possible.

This approach has kept the shop's original customers happy while continuing to draw in new fans who can't ignore the siren's song of chocolate bourbon pecan, banana cream, or apple crumb. Over the years, the couple has spread their wings to put new twists on standard items and expand their repertoire of savory offerings. Locals who swing by in the morning for a cup of Stumptown coffee can also grab a slice of the day's quiche or frittata, or a hand pie with egg, potato, and cheese (with or without sausage gravy).

Whole pies, small pies, and cinnamon rolls are available on a first come, first served basis on Fridays and Saturdays; special orders require from one to three days' notice. Because P is also for Patience.

2806 Corrine Dr.
407-745-4743
crazyforpies.com

Top: Diners can keep their eyes on the pie at all times. Photo by AaronVan.

Bottom left: Leave your worries behind. Photo by AaronVan.

Bottom right: Just a sprinkling of sugar finishes a lattice crust. Photo by AaronVan.

Seasonal American cuisine and pantry items

If you've ever gone to a restaurant and wondered whether you could re-create a dish at home, chef Ryan Freelove would like to give you a head start. Freelove not only makes all his restaurant's fresh beef and chicken broths, compound butters, clarified butter, salad dressings, and soups from scratch but also sells them at the Winter Garden Farmers Market so you can get one step closer to enjoying restaurant-quality cuisine at home.

You can still choose to let Freelove do the cooking at his downtown Winter Garden restaurant, where the seasonal dinner menu offers a mix of traditional yet elevated modern American dishes, such as a Florida Cattle Ranchers filet mignon with potato puree and red wine jus. The Central Florida native graduated from the Pennsylvania Institute for Culinary Arts and then spent two years exploring Austria's food and wine scene. Upon returning home, he worked with the area's top chefs at Victoria & Albert's, the Ritz Carlton Orlando, and the Peabody Orlando.

146 W. Plant St., Winter Garden
407-395-9871
market2table.com

"My favorite things we offer are our ingredients and all of our freshly made products, from Lake Meadow Naturals chicken to our house-made pasta and gnocchi, and all of our sauces and stocks."   – Ryan Freelove

Top: Berry macaron. Photo courtesy of Market to Table.

Bottom: Seasonal sip. Photo courtesy of Market to Table.

Table-to-farm experiences

The phrase "farm to table" has become so commonplace that many people have nearly forgotten how important that concept remains. Of course all food comes from some farm, somewhere, and smart corporate marketing types have applied "farm fresh" branding to food items with the same broad brush they use for "natural." In other words, the terms really don't mean much at all anymore. They should. It's crucial for folks to get outdoors to learn firsthand what thrives in their region and to appreciate the versatility and savor of authentically fresh ingredients, especially if those folks happen to be chefs.

At Grande Lakes Orlando, chefs needn't head out to the countryside to get their farm fix. They can wander over to Whisper Creek Farm, a seven-thousand-square-foot fruit and vegetable garden set amidst the resort's five-hundred-acre grounds. Products from the farm are featured at both of the hotels on the property, the Ritz-Carlton and the JW Marriott, where produce and fresh herbs pop up in restaurant dishes, beverages, and even spa treatments.

Taking the concept even further, guests can enjoy time on the farm as a family, with friends, or as part of a signature experience for couples. Families can take an extensive tour of the grounds before learning from the resort's farmers through a guided farming lesson. Everyone is able to sample the produce grown on-site and then enjoy a picnic lunch featuring many of those same farm-fresh—for-real—ingredients. The farm's greens might appear in a salad along with blistered beans and house-made bacon, or a skillet of cornbread may come slathered with honey from the farm's own hives.

Left: Whisper Creek Farm set up for an evening event. Photo courtesy of Grande Lakes Orlando.

Right: The entrance to Whisper Creek Farm. Photo courtesy of Grande Lakes Orlando.

Before heading to Highball & Harvest at the Ritz Carlton, couples can handpick their favorite ingredients to be incorporated into a special menu at the H&H Chef's Table. Herbs are infused into welcome cocktails, and a five-course meal with beverage pairings follows. At Whisper Creek Farm: The Kitchen, which is located at the JW Marriott, beer is an agricultural product too. Aaron Libera, the brewmaster at Whisper Creek Farm: The Brewery at the JW Marriott, offers an overview of how Whisper Creek Farm supports the brewery with a farm tour that highlights the fruits and herbs that fuel on-site beer production. After a visit to the Brewery, guests enjoy beer and bites at Whisper Creek Farm: The Kitchen.

Grande Lakes Orlando
4040 Central Florida Pkwy.
407-793-4683
grandelakes.com/whisper-creek-fables

RESTAURANTS A TO Z

1st Oriental Market, 116
5132 W. Colonial Dr.

1921 Mount Dora, 4
142 E. Fourth Ave.

A&M Provisions, 152
2816 Corrine Dr.

Ace Café Orlando, 166
100 W. Livingston St.

AJ's Press, 38
182 W. SR 434, Longwood

Anh Hong Restaurant, 120
1124 E. Colonial Dr.

Ararat Euro Food & Bistro, 186
7540 Universal Blvd.

Athena Roasted Chicken, 22
487 S. Orlando Ave.

**Audubon Park
Community Market, 10**
1842 E. Winter Park Rd.

Axum Coffee, 110
146 W. Plant St., Winter Garden
426 W. Plant St., Winter Garden
2000 Fowler Grove Blvd., Winter
   Garden

Bad As's Sandwich, 38
207 N. Primrose Dr.

Baggs Produce, 24
2485 Sanford Ave.

Banh Mi Nha Trang, 38
1216 E. Colonial Dr.

Beck Brothers, 146
12500 Overstreet Rd.,
   Windermere

Beefy King, 142
424 N. Bumby Ave.

Black Bean Deli, 118
1835 E. Colonial Dr.
325 S. Orlando Ave., Winter Park
1346 N. Orange Ave., Winter
   Park

The Black Hammock, 156
2316 Black Hammock
   Fish Camp Rd., Oviedo

Black Rooster Taqueria, 16
1323 N. Mills Ave.

The Boheme, 188
325 S. Orange Ave.

Buttermilk Bakery, 170
1198 Orange Ave., Winter Park

Canvas, 6
13615 Sachs Ave.

Capa, 192
10100 Dream Tree Blvd.

Caribbean Sunshine, 162
2528 W. Colonial Dr.
6922 Silver Star Rd.
16112 Marsh Rd., Winter
   Garden

The Catfish Place, 144
2324 Thirteenth St., St. Cloud

Central Florida Ale Trail, 126
Multiple locations

Ceviche House, 168
12213 S. Orange Blossom Tr.

Chapman's Berries, 146
75 Nolte Rd., St. Cloud

Chef Wang's Kitchen, 114
5148 W. Colonial Dr.

Christner's Prime
Steak and Lobster, 62
729 Lee Rd.

Claddagh Cottage Irish
Pub, 184
2421 Curry Ford Rd.

Claire Berries, 146
18751 Lake Pickett Rd.

The COOP, 82
610 W. Morse Blvd., Winter Park

Cuban Sandwiches to Go, 38
1605 Lee Rd.

DaJen Eats Café &
Creamery, 80
323 E. Kennedy Blvd.

Dandelion Community
Café, 42
618 N. Thornton Ave.

Digress, 56
1215 Edgewater Dr.

Disney Springs, 102
1486 E. Buena Vista Dr.

Dong A Supermarket, 120
812-816 Mills Ave.

DoveCote, 150
390 N. Orange Ave.

Downtown CREDO, 110
706 W. Smith St.
550 E. Rollins St.
885 N. Orange Ave.

East End Market, 2
3201 Corrine Dr.

Edible Education
Experience, 58
26 E. King St.

The Farmacy, 152
18 E. Joiner St., Winter Garden

Fleet Farming, 14
1030 Kaley Ave.

Gezellig Cookies, 28
See website for list of current
vendors.

The Goblin Market, 44
330 Dora Drawdy Way, Mount
Dora

Hanamizuki, 46
8255 International Dr.

Hollerbach's Willow Tree
Café, 164
205 E. First St., Sanford

Hollieanna Groves, 50
540 S. Orlando Ave., Maitland

Hoop-Dee-Doo Musical
Revue, 8
4510 N. Fort Wilderness Trail

Hoover's Market, 152
1035 Academy Dr., Altamonte
Springs

Hot Dog Heaven, 20
5355 E. Colonial Dr.

Hunger Street Tacos, 132
2103 W. Fairbanks Ave., Winter
Park

International Food Club, 172
4300 LB McLeod Rd.

Jimotti's Restaurant, 176
2545 S. French Ave., Sanford

Kadence, 196
1809 E. Winter Park Rd.

Kappy's Subs, 138
501 N. Orlando Ave., Maitland

King Grove Organic Farm, 146
19714 CR 44A, Eustis

Krungthep Tea Time, 160
1051 W. Fairbanks Ave., Winter
Park

Lake Meadow Naturals, 30
10000 Mark Adam Rd.

Lakeridge Winery &
Vineyards, 66
19239 US Hwy. 27 N., Clermont

A Land Remembered, 26
9939 Universal Blvd.

Lee & Rick's Oyster Bar, 136
5621 Old Winter Garden Rd.

Little Saigon Restaurant, 120
1106 E. Colonial Dr.

Long & Scott Farms, 108
26216 CR 448A, Mount Dora

Luisa's Cellar, 56
206 Sanford Ave., Sanford

Market to Table, 200
146 W. Plant St., Winter Garden

Maxine's on Shine, 154
337 N. Shine Ave.

The Meatball Stoppe, 68
7325 Lake Underhill Rd.

Melao Bakery, 174
2001 Consulate Dr.
1912 Fortune Rd., Kissimmee

Nile Ethiopian Restaurant, 46
7048 International Dr.

Norman's, 18
4012 Central Florida Pkwy.

Orlando Cat Café, 110
532 Cagan Park Ave., Clermont

Orlando Meats, 76
728 Virginia Dr.

P Is for Pie Bake Shop, 198
2806 Corrine Dr.

Palate Coffee Brewery, 110
105 W. Second St., Sanford

The Parkview, 56
136 S. Park Ave., Winter Park

Pho 88 Vietnamese
Restaurant, 120
730 N. Mills Ave.

Pizza Bruno, 128
3990 Curry Ford Rd.

Plant Street Market, 158
426 W. Plant St., Winter Garden

Prato, 140
124 N. Park Ave., Winter Park

Q'Kenan, 178
8117 Vineland Ave.

Rangoli Sweets, 74
370 E. SR 434, Winter Springs

The Ravenous Pig, 190
565 W. Fairbanks Ave., Winter
Park

Reel Fish Coastal
Kitchen + Bar, 134
1234 N. Orange Ave., Winter
Park

Reyes Mezcaleria, 194
821 N. Orange Ave.

The Rusty Spoon, 34
55 W. Church St.

Saba Bakes, 106
1255 Belle Ave. #172, Winter
Springs

The Sanctum, 60
715 N. Fern Creek Ave.

Sand Hill Blueberries, 146
31614 Bottany Woods Dr.,
Eustis

Se7en Bites, 52
617 N. Primrose Dr.

Selam Ethiopian & Eritrean Cuisine, 54
5494 Central Florida Pkwy.

Shantell's Just Until . . . , 12
503 S. Sanford Ave.

Shiraz Market, 72
185 S. Ronald Reagan Blvd.,
   Longwood

Showcase of Citrus, 50
5010 US Hwy. 27, Clermont

Soco Restaurant, 48
629 E. Central Blvd.

Southern Hill Farms, 146
16651 Schofield Rd., Clermont

Spicy Girl, 180
4311 W. Vine St., Kissimmee

A Spoon Full of Hope, 36

**Sticky Rice Lao Street
Food, 182**
1915 E. Colonial Dr.

Strong Water Tavern, 64
6601 Adventure Way

Sugar Rush Marshmallows, 112
See website for list of current
   vendors.

Swirlery Wine Bar, 56
1508 E. Michigan Ave.

Taipei 101, 32
3050 Alafaya Tr., Oviedo

Tapa Toro, 46
8441 International Dr.

Taste of Chengdu, 104
2030 W. Colonial Dr.

Taverna Opa, 46
9101 International Dr.

The Tennessee Truffle, 70
125 W. First St., Sanford

**Tien Hung Market Oriental
Food Center, 120**
1110 E. Colonial Dr.

Tom West Blueberries, 146
324 E. Orlando Ave., Ocoee

Tortas el Rey, 38
6151 S. Orange Blossom Tr.

Valhalla Bakery, 78
2603 E. South St.

Valkyrie Doughnuts, 78
160-12226 Corporate Blvd.

Victoria & Albert's, 122
4401 Floridian Way

Vietnam Cuisine, 120
1224 E. Colonial Dr.

The Whiskey, 130
7563 W. Sand Lake Rd.

Whisper Creek Farm, 202
4040 Central Florida Pkwy.

White's Red Hill Groves, 50
7218 Ronald Reagan Blvd.,
   Sanford

**Wild Hare Kitchen & Garden
Emporium, 152**
335 N. Ronald Reagan Blvd.,
   Longwood

**Winter Garden
Farmers Market, 124**
300 W. Plant St., Winter Garden

Wondermade Café, 112
214 E. First St., Sanford

ESTABLISHMENTS BY NEIGHBORHOOD

33RD STREET INDUSTRIAL

International Food Club, 172

ALTAMONTE SPRINGS

Hoover's Market, 152

AUDUBON PARK GARDEN DISTRICT

A&M Provisions, 152
Audubon Park Community
 Market, 10
East End Market, 2
Kadence, 196
P is for Pie Bake Shop, 198

CENTRAL BUSINESS DISTRICT

Ace Café Orlando, 166
The Boheme, 188
DoveCote, 150
The Rusty Spoon, 34

CLERMONT

Lakeridge Winery & Vineyards, 66
Orlando Cat Café, 110
Showcase of Citrus, 50
Southern Hill Farms, 146

COLLEGE PARK

Digress, 56
Downtown CREDO, 110
Edible Education Experience, 58

COLONIALTOWN CENTER

Bad As's Sandwich, 38
Hot Dog Heaven, 20
Se7en Bites, 52

COLONIALTOWN NORTH

The Sanctum, 60
Sticky Rice Lao Street Food, 182

COLONIALTOWN SOUTH

Beefy King, 142
Maxine's on Shine, 154

CONWAY

Claddagh Cottage Irish Pub, 184
Pizza Bruno, 128
Swirlery Wine Bar, 56

DOCTOR PHILLIPS

The Whiskey, 130

EAST CENTRAL PARK

Valhalla Bakery, 78

EATONVILLE

DaJen Eats Café & Creamery, 80

EUSTIS

King Grove Organic Farm, 146
Sand Hill Blueberries, 146

FAIRVIEW SHORES

Christner's Prime Steak and
  Lobster, 62
Cuban Sandwiches to Go, 38

HUNTER'S GREEK

Melao Bakery, 174

I-DRIVE AREA

Ararat Euro Food & Bistro, 186
Hanamizuki, 46
Nile Ethiopian Restaurant, 46
Tapa Toro, 46
Taverna Opa, 46

KISSIMMEE

Melao Bakery, 174
Spicy Girl, 180

LAKE NONA

Canvas, 6

LAKE UNDERHILL

The Meatball Stoppe, 68

LONGWOOD

AJ's Press, 38
Shiraz Market, 72
Wild Hare Kitchen & Garden
  Emporium, 152

MAITLAND

Athena Roasted Chicken, 22
Hollieanna Groves, 50
Kappy's Subs, 138

MILLS 50 DISTRICT

Anh Hong Restaurant, 120
Banh Mi Nha Trang, 38
Black Bean Deli, 118
Black Rooster Taqueria, 16
Dong A Supermarket, 120
Little Saigon Restaurant, 120
Orlando Meats, 76
Pho 88 Vietnamese
  Restaurant, 120
Vietnam Cuisine, 120

MOUNT DORA

1921 Mount Dora, 4
Long & Scott Farms, 108
The Goblin Market, 44

NORTH QUARTER

Downtown CREDO, 110
Reyes Mezcaleria, 194

ORANGE BLOSSOM TRAIL

Ceviche House, 168
Tortas el Rey, 38

OCOEE

Lake Meadow Naturals, 30
Tom West Blueberries, 146

ORLOVISTA

1st Oriental Market, 116
Chef Wang's Kitchen, 114
Lee & Rick's Oyster Bar, 136

OVIEDO

The Black Hammock, 156
Taipei 101, 32

PINE HILLS

Caribbean Sunshine, 162

RESORTS AREA

4 Rivers Cantina Barbacoa Food
  Truck, 102
Chef Art Smith's Homecomin', 102
Capa, 192
Hoop-Dee-Doo Musical Revue, 8
A Land Remembered, 26
The Polite Pig, 102
Strong Water Tavern, 64
Victoria & Albert's, 122
Whisper Creek Farm, 202
Wine Bar George, 102

SANFORD

Baggs Produce, 24
Hollerbach's Willow Tree Café, 164
Jimotti's Restaurant, 176
Luisa's Cellar, 56
Magnolia Square Market, 165
Palate Coffee Brewery, 110
Shantell's Just Until . . . , 12
The Tennessee Truffle, 70
White's Red Hill Groves, 50
Wondermade Café, 112

ST. CLOUD

The Catfish Place, 144
Chapman's Berries, 146

THORNTON PARK

Soco Restaurant, 48

UCF

Claire Berries, 146
Valkyrie Doughnuts, 78

WEST COLONIAL

Caribbean Sunshine, 162
Taste of Chengdu, 104

WILLIAMSBURG

Q'Kenan, 178
Selam Ethiopian & Eritrean
  Cuisine, 54

WINDERMERE

Beck Brothers, 146

WINTER GARDEN

Axum Coffee, 110
Caribbean Sunshine, 162
The Farmacy, 152
Market to Table, 200
Plant Street Market, 158
Winter Garden Farmers
  Market, 124

WINTER PARK

Black Bean Deli, 118
Buttermilk Bakery, 170
The COOP, 82
Hunger Street Tacos, 132
Krungthep Tea Time, 160
The Parkview, 56
Prato, 140
The Ravenous Pig, 190
Reel Fish Coastal Kitchen
  + Bar, 134

WINTER SPRINGS

Rangoli Sweets, 74
Saba Bakes, 106